A Treasure Trove of Olde Recipes

Lost in an attic
May quite a find----
These treasured recipes
Of every kind.

Covered with dust
as years went by--
Green Tomatoe Pickle
Transparent Pie.

Gathered Together
You will see----
White House Punch
And Russian Tea

Also pickles and puddings
from sour To sweet---
A Treasure-Trove
Of quaint things To eat.

Found in an Olde Attic

By:
J. Eugene Orr
Hugh Hackett Pratt
Lee Montgomery Pratt - Artist

20th November 1971

To Elaine Tucker :

May you find many hours of
joy in the art of cooking
"ole Timey Southern Style.

Sincerely
Lee Montgomery Pratt

Something of Value .....

One Saturday afternoon the editors of this book visited a small, almost vanishing country town to look for antiques which was their hobby. The town, almost 200 years old, had evolved from an original land grant from King Charles of England to a prosperous farm village. However, during the last 40 years the town's population had dwindled to a population of a few hundred people, and not a soul could be seen walking on the sidewalks after 5:30 in the afternoon.

There are some small shops still open in the town. Two grocery stores and a second hand furniture store command most of the business. It was the custom of these old stores to store all the goods they could not sell years ago in the attic. Therefore, today one rummaging in the attic of one of these old stores might find old coffins, high top shoes, horse collars, and many other things.

It was in one of these old attics where the treasure-trove of recipes were found. They were in an old box way over in a corner of the attic and had been there for many years. A treasure-trove is a treasure found hidden or a valuable discovery. It is our belief that these recipes have been handed down from generation to generation as is the custom and are........
Something of Value

Dedications:

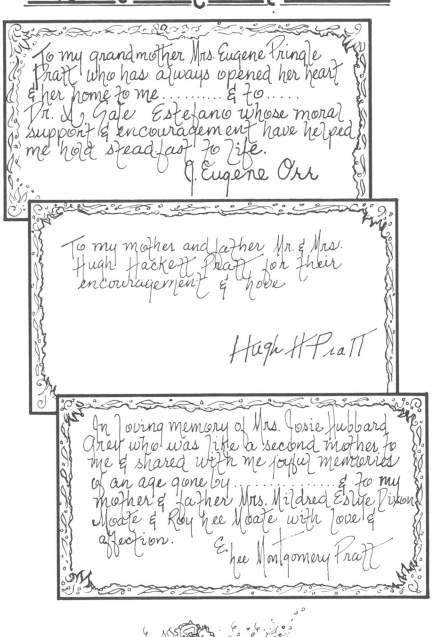

To my grandmother Mrs. Eugene Pringle Pratt who has always opened her heart & her home to me.......... & to...... Dr. A. Gale Estefano whose moral support & encouragement have helped me hold steadfast to life.

J. Eugene Orr

To my mother and father Mr. & Mrs. Hugh Hackett Pratt for their encouragement & hope

Hugh H. Pratt

In loving memory of Mrs. Josie Hubbard Grey who was like a second mother to me & shared with me joyful memories of an age gone by.............. & to my mother & father Mrs. Mildred Eslye Dixon Moate & Roy Lee Moate with love & affection.

E. Lee Montgomery Pratt

Our Special Thanks To:

Mrs. May Haynsworth Bull and her dear mother, Mrs. Ida May Guess Haynsworth, our neighbors, whose knowledge of things past was invaluable in helping us to interpret many of these old recipes.........

Gion Cassoni, a fellow artist, whose encouragement turned a dream into reality.........

Mrs. Faye Spires Price and her sister, Mrs. Carolyn Spires Mitchum, who gave us their assistance when energy was ebbing low.........

Mrs. May Darby, our maid, who assumed a mother's responsibilities and more in order that this book could be completed without delay.........

And all the people too numerous to name who have eagerly waited for this book to be published.

The Editors

The Table of Contents

Cookies continued:

Pies:

Puddings & Assorted Desserts

puddings & Assorted Desserts contd:

Beverages:

Candies:

Vegetables & Casseroles:

Vegetables & Casseroles continued:

Sauces:

Salads:

Meat, Fish, & Poultry

Meat, Fish & Poultry continued: Page

Universal Pickles

To one (1) gallon vinegar add:

    ½ pt. (pint) salt
    2 oz. pickle spice
    2 oz. ginger
    2 oz. black pepper
    1 lb. brown sugar
    1 large box mustard
    1 oz of white mustard seed
    3 or 4 large onions (cut in half)

Stir until all ingredients are mixed well. Fill the jar with sliced cucumbers, cabbage, and green tomatoes... stir frequently and keep vegetables well covered with vinegar.

Mixed Sweet Pickles

4 qts. green tomatoes   2 medium cabbages
2 pounds onions   2 or 3 hot peppers
1 doz. green, or ten green and 2 red (sweet) peppers
Grind through course meat chopper. Soak over night
in brine (1 gal. water and 1 cup salt) Drain next
morning and put in the following sauce and cook for
30 minutes, boiling and stirring all the time. Sauce:
5 Tbsp. dry mustard   1 Tbsp. tumeric
1 Tbsp. celery seed   1 teasp. black pepper
2 quarts vinegar   5 cups brown sugar & 1½ cups flour
                                   (mixed)
Mix dry ingredients and add vinegar slowly. Cook
until thick. Then add vegetables and cook 30 minutes.
Put in jars and seal.

Green Tomatoe Sweet Pickles

8 lbs. green tomatoes   4 lbs brown sugar
Chop tomatoes fine, add brown sugar &
boil down 3 hours.   Add
1 quart vinegar   1 teap. each of
mace, cinnamon, cloves - Boil about
15 minutes. Cool. Put into jars & seal.

Peach Sweet Pickles

4 quarts peaches   1½ pints vinegar
3 or 4 sticks cinnamon Whole Cloves
2 lbs. sugar (brown sugar preferred)

Have your peaches (press or cling variety is best) peeled or skins removed by dipping them in boiling water and rubbing off skins with cloth.

Make a syrup of the sugar and vinegar dropping in the cinnamon sticks cooking them together for 20 minutes.

Stick two cloves into each peach and cook them in the syrup (a few peaches at the time) till tender.

Boil syrup for 10 minutes after all the fruit is done, then pour it over the peaches which have been placed carefully with spoon in sterilized jars. Seal.

Pear Pickles

12 Fresh Pears   12 red sweet peppers
1 cup onions   2 Tbsp. salt
5 cups vinegar   2 cups sugar
2 whole gloves per each pear   1 Tbsp. pickle spice

Peel and core pears then grind them coarse
Core and cut red peppers into small pieces
Cut onions medium fine. Blend pears,
peppers, and onions with salt and drain
for one hour. Heat vinegar and sugar to
boiling point. Slowly add drained ingredients
Simmer for 20 minutes. Add cloves and
spice. Pack in Jars.

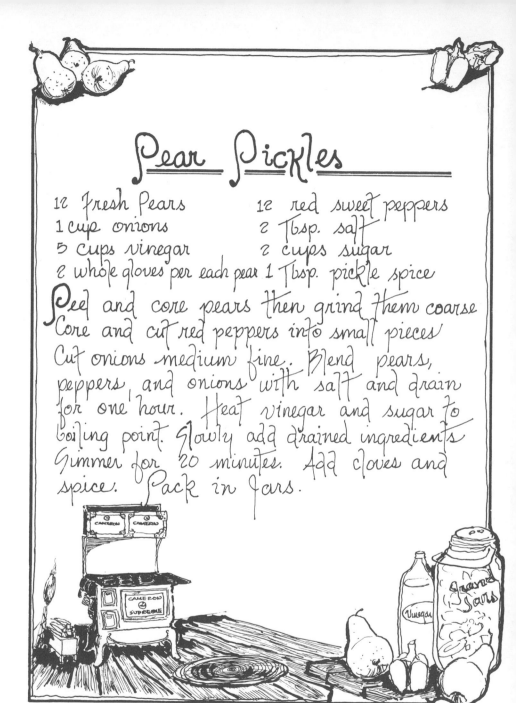

Cauliflower Pickles

2 heads cauliflower   1 large bunch celery
3 medium size cabbages 6 or 8 big onions
4 quarts of water & 1 pint salt mixed (brine)

Chop all vegetables fine, except onions, and
let stand over night in brine.
Drain vegetables next day, add onions
and put in kettle. Pour dressing
over and cook for about 10 minutes.

DRESSING:
1 cup flour   1 quart vinegar
2 pounds of white sugar

Mix ingredients with a little of the
vinegar. Stir until smooth then add
remaining vinegar. Mix well and
pour in kettle as instructed above.

Watermelon Rind Pickles

1 Pound rind after it has been prepared
4 cups sugar   1 cup water
3 cups vinegar   1 Tbsp. whole spices

Remove the green and pink parts of the rind and cut it into the desired size and shape. Weigh the rind and cover with salt water, allowing one tablespoon of salt to each quart of water. Let stand overnight then drain, rinse rind in cold water, and drain again. Mix sugar water, vinegar and whole spices in large kettle. Cook pieces of rind a few at a time until transparent. Place pieces in sterilized jars. When all rinds have been prepared, boil syrup 10 minutes longer and pour over rind pickles in jars. Seal.

Mustard Pickles

1 quart sm. white onions 1 quart sliced cucumbers
1 quart whole small cucumbers
4 large green peppers (chopped)
1 large head cauliflower
4 quarts water   1 pint salt

Make brine of water and salt. Soak onions and cucumbers together, peppers separately, in brine for 12 to 24 hours.

Drain very dry the next day. Steam cauliflower slightly after preparing the following:

DRESSING:

1 cup flour   6 Tbsp. dry mustard
1 Tbsp. Tumeric   1 cup sugar

Vinegar (cold) enough added to the above ingredients to equal 2 quarts in all.

Mix and boil to a smooth paste stirring constantly. Add onions, cucumbers, and peppers. Cook until heated thoroughly, then stir in the hot cauliflower. Seal

Grand Jan

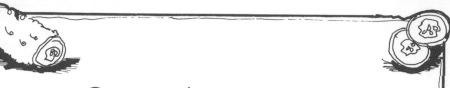

Cucumber Pickles I

1 peck cucumbers   2 cups salt
1 gal. water (NOTE: Soak whole cucumbers unpeeled)

Soak cucumbers in solution of 2 cups salt to 1 gallon of water for one week

1 cup unslaked lime   1 gal. water

Rinse cucumbers and put in solution of water and unslaked lime for 3 or 4 hours. (Peel and slice cucumbers before putting in lime water if desired.) Remove from lime water and rinse well. (lime makes a crisper pickle.)

½ box whole spice - 1 cup sugar to every cup vinegar used

3 qts. to 1 gallon vinegar (enough to cover the cucumbers.)

Mix whole spice, vinegar, and sugar and let come to a boil. Pour over cucumbers and let stand overnight. Pour syrup off and boil 10 min. Pour back on. let stand 2 hours more. then put all on stove and boil 10 minutes. Put in sterilized jars and seal.

Cucumber Pickles II

12 sliced cucumbers   2 cups vinegar
1 cup water   1 cup sugar
1 teasp. whole spice   ½ teasp. mustard seed

Slice cucumbers but not too thin. Soak overnight in a cold water brine of one cup salt to one gallon of water.

Drain good next day and make syrup of vinegar, water, sugar, whole spice, and mustard seed. Bring to boil then add the cucumbers. Boil about three minutes until they lose green look. Pack pickles solidly into sterilized jars. Add 1 teaspoon salt and ½ onion sliced to each quart. Cover with boiling syrup and seal.

Uncooked Relish

1 carrot	1 onion
1 tomatoe	1 green pepper
1 red pepper	1 tart apple

Put through food chopper. Season to taste with lemon juice, mayonnaise, salt and pepper.

Chow Chow

4 qts. of green tomatoes   2 qts. of cabbage
1 qt. of onions   4 green and red peppers(mixed)
1 Tbsp. of allspice   1 Tbsp. of cloves
1 Tbsp. of cinnamon   2 Tbsp. of mustard
2 Tbsp. of tumeric   1 cup sugar
2 qts. good cider vinegar. Salt to taste

Mix all ingredients thoroughly and boil for
one hour. Seal in sterilized jars.

Pepper Hash

12 large red peppers 12 large green peppers
15 medium sized onions

Put through medium knife food chopper.
Cover with boiling water and let stand
10 minutes. Drain until quite
dry. Add 3½ cupfuls vinegar,
1½ cupfuls sugar and 3
tablespoonfuls salt. Boil
15 minutes, pack in sterilized jars &
seal. (NOTE:) Can also use 1 small cabbage
ground, but don't put boiling water on it.

Pepper Relish

12 large red sweet peppers   12 large green sweet peppers
1 pod hot pepper   9 medium onions
1 cup sugar   1 Tbsp. salt
2 cups vinegar   1 Tbsp. mixed spices
12 cups of boiling water

Remove seeds and membrane from sweet peppers and peel onions (Use whole hot pepper). Chop peppers and onions. Drain Cover "pepper-onion mixture" with 6 cups boiling water. Let stand 5 minutes. Drain. Cover with remaining 6 cups boiling water. Let stand 10 minutes. Drain. Tie spices in a cheese-cloth bag. Add sugar, salt, vinegar, and spices. Simmer 15 minutes. Remove bag of spices. Pack hot relish in hot pint jars. Seal at once. Makes 4 pints.

Pear Relish

4 qts pears   3 cups vinegar
½ small onion   2 teasps. pickle spice
½ teasp whole cloves 2½ cups sugar

Pare and grind the pears. Use coarse blade
of grinder. Drain juice from pears. Leave
just enough juice to start pears boiling.
Add salt to taste (1 teasp.) Boil pears till
tender. When pears are nearly done, heat
vinegar in another vessel along with
sugar, onion, and spices. When vinegar is
at boiling, dip pears from juice, put into
vessel of vinegar mixture, stir, and bring to
boiling point. Put into sterilized jars
and seal. (Cook vinegar in agate vessel
if possible.)

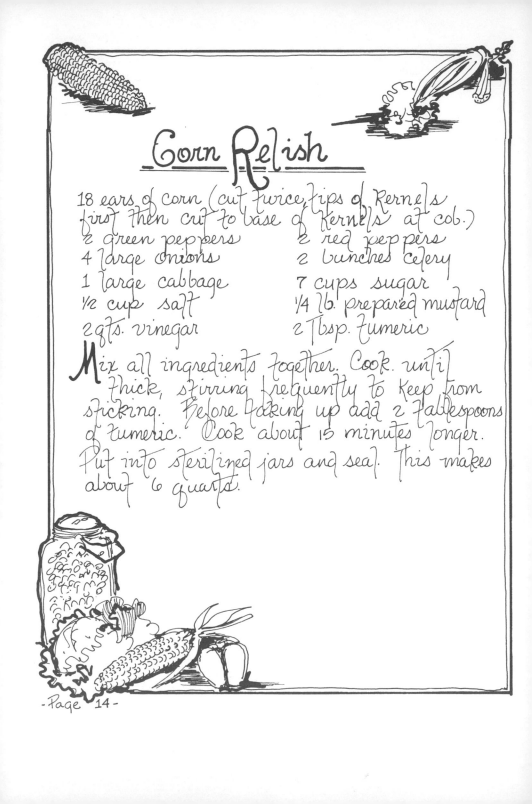

Corn Relish

18 ears of corn (cut twice, tips of Kernels
first then cut to base of Kernels at cob.)
2 green peppers   2 red peppers
4 large onions   2 bunches celery
1 large cabbage   7 cups sugar
½ cup salt   ¼ lb. prepared mustard
2 qts. vinegar   2 Tbsp. Tumeric

Mix all ingredients together. Cook until
thick, stirring frequently to keep from
sticking. Before taking up add 2 Tablespoons
of Tumeric. Cook about 15 minutes longer.
Put into sterilized jars and seal. This makes
about 6 quarts.

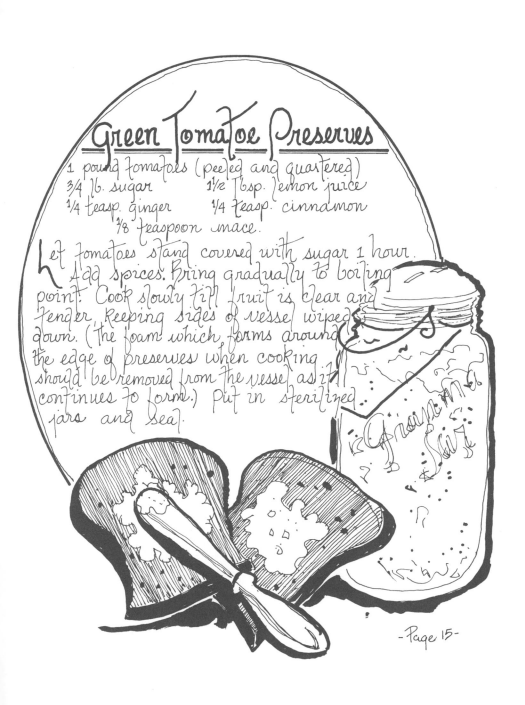

Green Tomatoe Preserves

1 pound tomatoes (peeled and quartered)
3/4 lb. sugar   1½ Tbsp. lemon juice
¼ teasp. ginger   ¼ teasp. cinnamon
⅛ teaspoon mace.

Let tomatoes stand covered with sugar 1 hour. Add spices. Bring gradually to boiling point. Cook slowly till fruit is clear and tender, keeping sides of vessel wiped down. (The foam which forms around the edge of preserves when cooking should be removed from the vessel as it continues to form.) Put in sterilized jars and seal.

Pear Honey

8 lbs. pears   4 lbs sugar
4 oranges   1 can pineapple (#2)

Grind pears in meat chopper, add sugar and boil until looks clear. Then add pineapple ground and oranges ground. (Note: 10 lbs. of pears can be used and I think it plenty sweet.)

Pear Mince Meat (for Pie also)

8 lbs pears ground (medium)   1 lb. raisins
4 oranges, 2 ground medium, 2 ground fine
2 lemons   3½ lbs. sugar (brown preferred)
1 teasp. nutmeg   1 teasp. cinnamon
1 teasp. allspice   ½ teasp. ginger
½ teasp. cloves   1 quart fig preserves

Put all in sauce pan and boil 1 hour, adding fig preserves after other ingredients start boiling. Seal in pint jars. Makes 6 or 8 pints. This makes a grand pie served with whipped cream.

Note: Remove foam which forms around edges of cooking preserves for best results.

Pear Harlequin

6 lbs. pears

sugar (¾ quantity)

2 oranges

1 can pineapple (large broken pieces)

½ pint bottle maraschino cherries

Wipe pears, stem, core and cut in small pieces. Add pineapple and oranges. Measure. Add three-fourths quantity of sugar. Let stand overnight. Simmer until thick. Cut cherries in half and add with liquid in bottle. Stir well. Fill sterilized jars, seal, label & store. Makes 6 pints.

Pear Marmalade

8 cups of pears (ground)

2 cups of grated coconut

3 oranges (ground)

2 cups grated pineapple

8 cups sugar

Peel pears and put through food chopper. Peel oranges and put through food chopper, using only half of peel. Mix pears, oranges, and sugar. Cook until pears are clear. Add grated pineapple & grated coconut. Let come to boil. Seal in sterilized jars.

Note: Remove foam which forms around cooking preserves for best results.

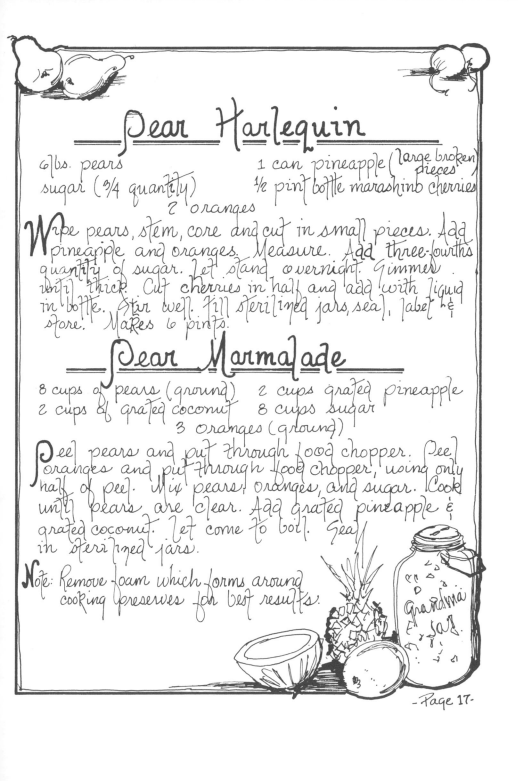

Spiced Grapes

5 lbs. grapes   3 lbs. sugar
2 teasp. allspice   1 cup vinegar
2 teasp. cinnamon   ½ teasp. cloves

Pulp grapes. Boil skins until tender. Add pulp. Cook until tender. Run through sieve. Add sugar, spices, and vinegar. Boil till right consistency. Cool. Seal in sterilized jars.

Cranberry Sauce

1 qt. cranberries   4 cups sugar
            4 cups water.

Boil water and sugar 20 minutes. Skim. Add cranberries which have been well washed and picked and drained. Boil 5 minutes or until all berries have popped. Seal in sterilized jars.

Note: Remove foam which forms around cooking preserves for best results.

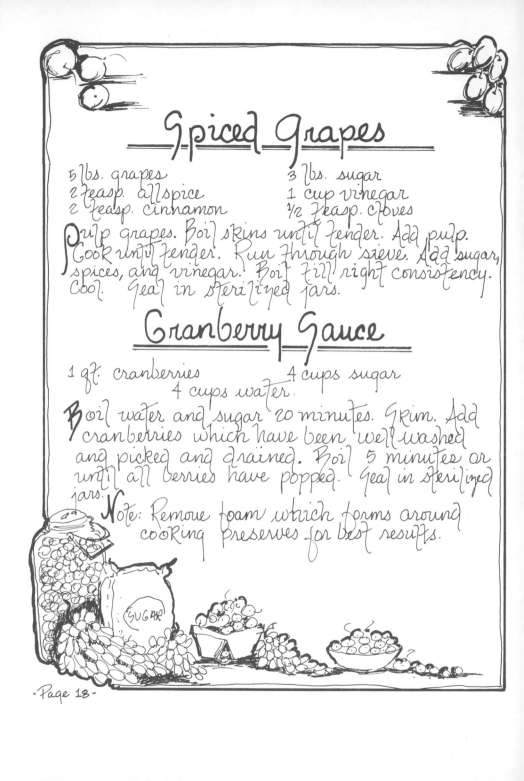

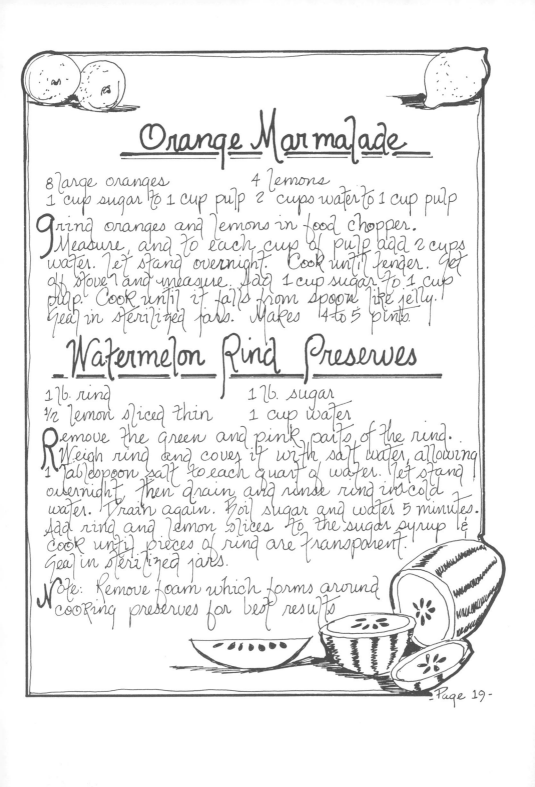

Orange Marmalade

8 large oranges   4 lemons
1 cup sugar to 1 cup pulp   2 cups water to 1 cup pulp

Grind oranges and lemons in food chopper.
Measure, and to each cup of pulp add 2 cups
water. Let stand overnight. Cook until tender. Get
off stove and measure. Add 1 cup sugar to 1 cup
pulp. Cook until it falls from spoon like jelly.
Seal in sterilized jars. Makes 4 to 5 pints.

Watermelon Rind Preserves

1 lb. rind   1 lb. sugar
½ lemon sliced thin   1 cup water

Remove the green and pink parts of the rind.
Weigh rind and cover it with salt water, allowing
1 tablespoon salt to each quart of water. Let stand
overnight, then drain and rinse rind in cold
water. Drain again. Boil sugar and water 5 minutes.
Add rind and lemon slices to the sugar syrup &
cook until pieces of rind are transparent.
Seal in sterilized jars.

Note: Remove foam which forms around
cooking preserves for best results

Nut Bread

3 cups sifted flour   1 cup sugar
1 cup chopped nuts   3 teasp. baking powder
1 teasp. salt   1 tabsp. shortening
1 cup milk   1 egg

Mix dry ingredients. Let stand 20 minutes on stove before baking. Bake in moderate oven (350°F) 1 hour. Omit shortening if black walnuts are used. Cuts better if a day old.

Ginger Bread

1½ cups New Orleans molasses
3 cups flour (sifted)   ½ cup boiling water
¼ cup butter   1 teasp. soda
2 teasp. ginger   1 teasp. salt

Add soda, ginger and salt to sifted flour and re-sift. Add hot water to molasses and combine this with flour mixture. Add the butter and beat to firm, smooth batter. Pour in greased pan and bake in moderate (350°F.) oven for half an hour. Top with boiled icing if desired.

Ice Box Rolls

1 cup milk
3 Tbsp. sugar
1 yeast cake

3 Tbsp. shortening
1 teasp. salt
1 egg

2 ¾ to 3 cups flour

Scald milk and dissolve shortening, sugar, & salt in it. While mixture is warm, add yeast cake crumbled and egg. Add flour gradually and mix thoroughly by beating. Let rise until double in bulk. Place dough in bowl and cover with waxed paper which is held over bowl with a rubber band. Store in ice box until ready for use. This dough may be used for cloverleaf rolls, cinnamon braid, fruit-filled rings, or pecan rolls.

(350° F)

Pop-Overs

1 cup flour   7/8 cup milk
1/4 teasp. salt   2 eggs
        1/2 teasp. melted butter

Mix salt and flour. Add milk gradually to make a smooth batter. Beat whole eggs until light and add to mixture. Add butter. Beat 2 minutes with egg beater. Turn into buttered custard cups or hissing hot buttered iron gem pans (muffin tins). Bake 30 to 35 minutes beginning with hot oven 450°F, decreasing gradually to a moderate oven of 350°F. as pop-overs start to brown. Note: Thorough beating and correct baking are the secrets of perfect pop-overs.

Pitts Rolls

3 Tbsp. shortening
1 teaspoon salt
1 yeast cake
1 egg

¼ cup sugar
⅔ cup sweet milk (heated)
¼ cup warm water
3½ cups flour

Cream shortening, sugar and salt and add heated milk. Let cool. Dissolve yeast cake in warm water and add to mixture. Add egg and mix well. Then stir in flour and let rise for 2 hours. Roll out and cut into buns. Place on greased baking sheet and bake in hot oven.

Hot Rolls I

3 cups flour
1 yeast cake
1½ cup hot water
1 egg

½ cup lard
½ cup cold water
½ cup sugar
½ teasp. salt

Cream lard and sugar together. Add ½ cup hot water. Add ½ cup cold water with yeast dissolved in it. Add egg beaten lightly. Have salt and flour sifted together. Add this to the mixture. Make up and put in ice box. When ready to use put in muffin tins. Let rise and bake in hot oven.

Hot Rolls II

1 cup scalded milk   1 cup mashed potatoes
1/2 cup shortening   1 teasp. salt
1/2 cup sugar   1 yeast cake (or package)
1/2 cup warm water   1 egg
6 to 8 cups flour

Scald milk and lard together. Dissolve yeast cake and sugar in warm water. Beat egg. Combine these ingredients. Add salt and potatoes. Then add the flour to a kneading consistency. Place in a greased bowl. Cover and let rise to double its size. Then pinch off in rolls and bake in hot oven.

Potatoe Rolls

6 to 7 cups flour   1 cup mashed boiled Irish potatoes
3/4 cup lard   1 cup milk
2 eggs well-beaten   1/2 scant cup sugar
salt to taste
1 cake compressed yeast dissolved in 1/2 cup luke warm water.

Mix 1 cup flour with lard, potatoes, sugar, salt and eggs. Next add milk, then dissolved yeast. Let to rise for 2 hours. Make into a soft dough by adding remaining 5 or 6 cups of flour and set to rise again. Shape, let rise and bake in a hot oven.

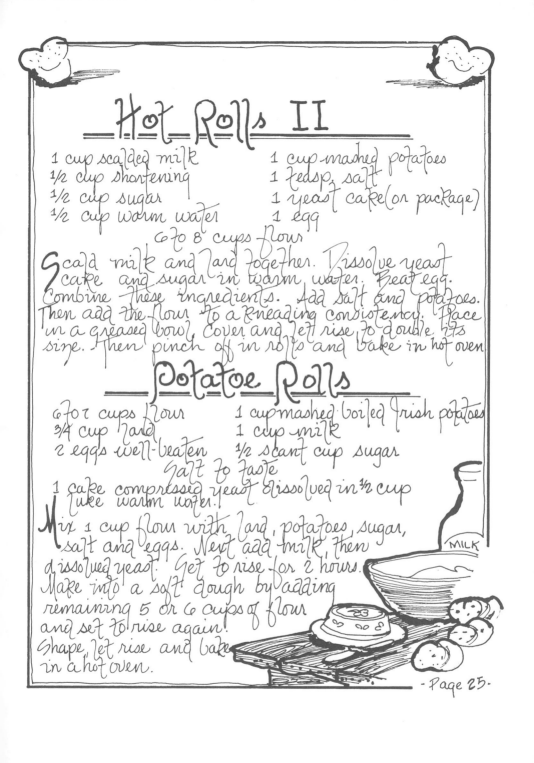

Hot Biscuits

2 cups self-rising flour (sifted) 1 teasp. soda
Shortening (size of two eggs)
buttermilk (enough to make soft dough)
Add soda to flour. Make hole in flour with
hand and work in shortening. When well
creamed, mix in enough buttermilk to make
soft dough. Then work in enough extra flour
to make firm dough. Roll out to about half an
inch thick and cut biscuits with round
cutter. Bake in a very hot oven and serve hot.

All-Bran Muffins

2 Tbsp. shortening   1/4 cup sugar
1 egg   1 cup sour milk
1 cup all-bran   1 cup flour
  1/2 teasp. soda   1 teasp. baking powder
      1/2 teasp. salt.
    Cream   shortening and sugar. Add
             egg and beat well. Add
             milk and all-bran. Mix
             and sift dry ingredients
             and add to mixture. Bake
               in greased muffin tins
                in moderate oven
                 for about 30 minutes

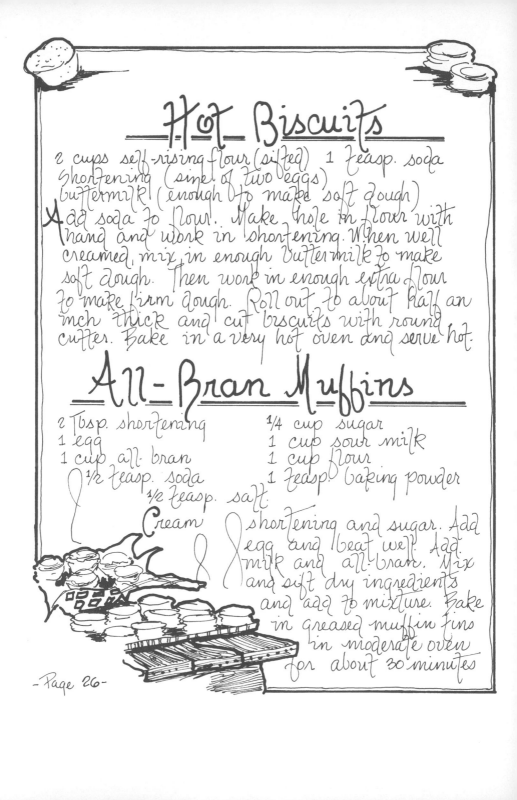

Corn Bread Sticks

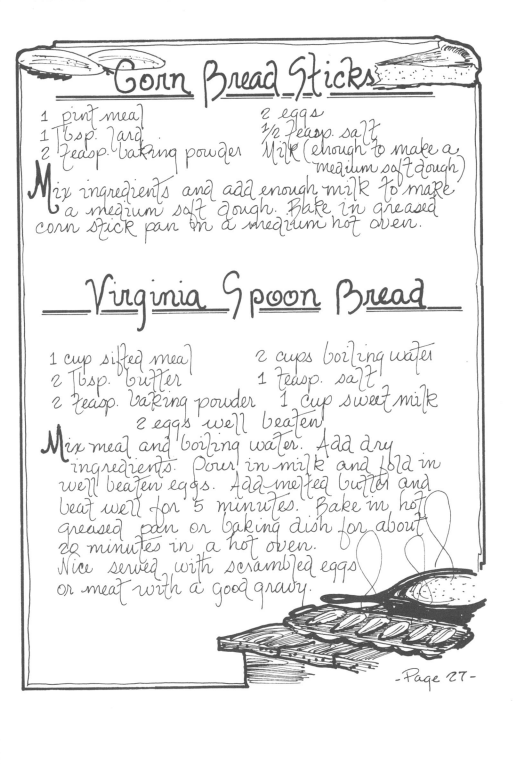

1 pint meal
1 Tbsp. lard
2 Teasp. baking powder

2 eggs
1/2 Teasp. salt
Milk (enough to make a
medium soft dough)

Mix ingredients and add enough milk to make a medium soft dough. Bake in greased corn stick pan in a medium hot oven.

Virginia Spoon Bread

1 cup sifted meal
2 Tbsp. butter
2 Teasp. baking powder
2 eggs well beaten

2 cups boiling water
1 Teasp. salt
1 cup sweet milk

Mix meal and boiling water. Add dry ingredients. Pour in milk and fold in well beaten eggs. Add melted butter and beat well for 5 minutes. Bake in hot greased pan or baking dish for about 22 minutes in a hot oven.
Nice served with scrambled eggs or meat with a good gravy.

Hush Puppies I

1 small onion chopped fine - 2 cups yellow corn meal
½ cup flour   dash of salt

Mix chopped onion, corn meal, flour and salt. Moisten with water. Mold into balls an inch in diameter and drop into smoking hot fat in which fish were fried. An egg stirred into dough improves the hush puppies.

Hush Puppies II or Red Horse Bread

2 cups enriched corn meal   1 Tbsp. enriched flour
1 Teasp. soda   1 Teaspoon baking power
1 Tbsp. salt   1 whole egg
6 Tbsp. chopped onion   2 cups buttermilk

Mix all dry ingredients, add chopped onion, then milk and egg. Drop by spoonfuls into deep hot grease where fish are cooking. When done they will float. Put on brown paper to drain.

Red Horse bread is made in a quite similar manner -- the onion may be omitted. If eggs are plentiful the milk & the baking powder are left out. Use enough eggs to make a batter. No "fish-fry" is complete without Hush Puppies or Red Horse Bread.

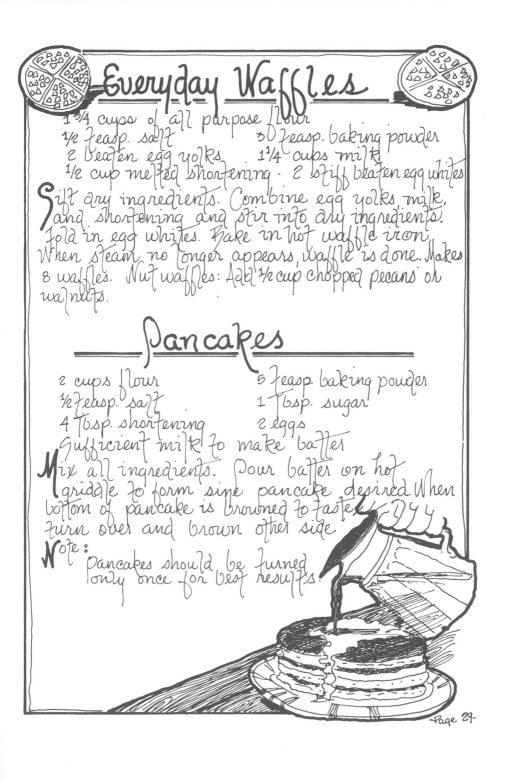

Everyday Waffles

1¾ cups of all purpose flour
½ Teasp. salt   3 Teasp. baking powder
2 beaten egg yolks   1¼ cups milk
½ cup melted shortening · 2 stiff beaten egg whites

Sift dry ingredients. Combine egg yolks, milk, and shortening and stir into dry ingredients. Fold in egg whites. Bake in hot waffle iron. When steam no longer appears, waffle is done. Makes 8 waffles. Nut waffles: Add ½ cup chopped pecans or walnuts.

Pancakes

2 cups flour   5 Teasp. baking powder
½ Teasp. salt   1 Tbsp. sugar
4 Tbsp. shortening   2 eggs
Sufficient milk to make batter

Mix all ingredients. Pour batter on hot griddle to form size pancake desired. When bottom of pancake is browned to taste, turn over and brown other side.

Note: Pancakes should be turned only once for best results.

The Cake That..

2/3 cup shortening
3 eggs
1½ cups sugar
2/3 cup cocoa
½ cup hot water
2 teasp. baking powder
1 cup thick sour milk
½ teasp. soda
1 teasp. vanilla
2 cups flour
1 teasp. salt

Goes to Church

Blend shortening, sugar, and eggs in one operation. Beat cocoa into hot water until smooth and add to first mixture. Sift flour, salt and baking powder together and add to sugar mixture alternately with the milk to which has been added the soda & flavoring. Bake in three greased 8-inch layer cake pans in moderate oven (350°F.) for about 20 or so minutes. (thin layers) When cool put layers with the following icing:

1¾ cups granulated sugar - ⅛ teasp. salt
½ cup water   3 egg whites
          & 12 marshmallows cut into pieces

Mix sugar, salt, and water and cook to a soft ball stage when dropped into cold water. (238°F.). Pour slowly over egg whites which have been beaten stiff, beating mixture as you do so. While icing is still hot, fold in cut marshmallows. Beat until of a consistency to spread. All measurements are level.

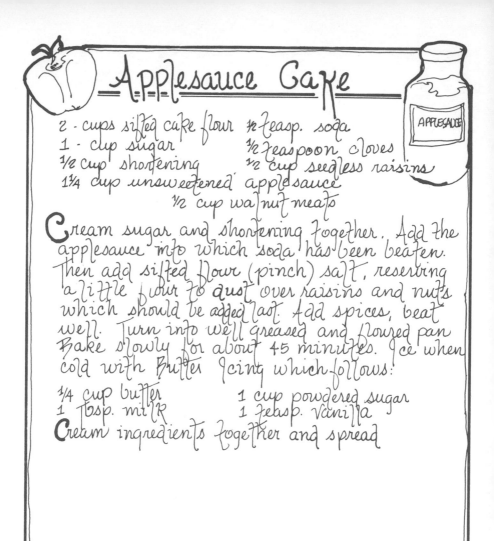

Applesauce Cake

2 - cups sifted cake flour   ½ teasp. soda
1 - cup sugar   ½ teaspoon cloves
½ cup shortening   ½ cup seedless raisins
1¼ cup unsweetened applesauce
½ cup walnut meats

Cream sugar and shortening together. Add the applesauce into which soda has been beaten. Then add sifted flour (pinch) salt, reserving a little flour to dust over raisins and nuts which should be added last. Add spices, beat well. Turn into well greased and floured pan Bake slowly for about 45 minutes. Ice when cold with Butter Icing which follows:

¼ cup butter   1 cup powdered sugar
1 Tbsp. milk   1 teasp. vanilla
Cream ingredients together and spread

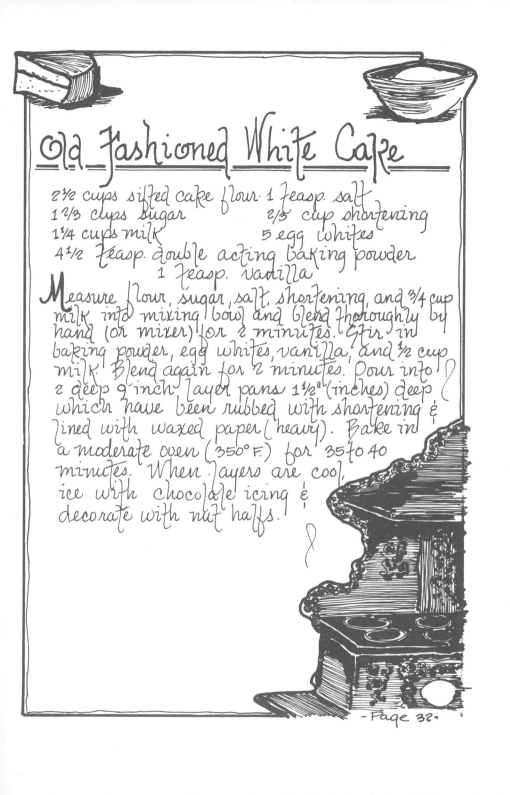

Old Fashioned White Cake

2½ cups sifted cake flour · 1 teasp. salt
1⅔ cups sugar   ⅔ cup shortening
1¼ cups milk   5 egg whites
4½ teasp. double acting baking powder
1 teasp. vanilla

Measure flour, sugar, salt, shortening, and ¾ cup milk into mixing bowl and blend thoroughly by hand (or mixer) for 2 minutes. Stir in baking powder, egg whites, vanilla, and ½ cup milk. Blend again for 2 minutes. Pour into 2 deep 9 inch layer pans 1½" (inches) deep which have been rubbed with shortening & lined with waxed paper (heavy). Bake in a moderate oven (350° F.) for 35 to 40 minutes. When layers are cool, ice with chocolate icing & decorate with nut halfs.

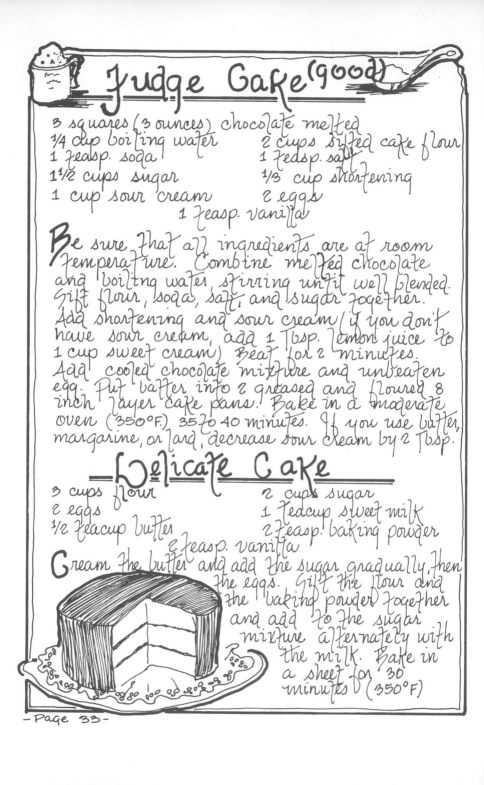

Fudge Cake (good)

3 squares (3 ounces) chocolate melted
¼ cup boiling water   2 cups sifted cake flour
1 teasp. soda   1 teasp. salt
1½ cups sugar   ⅓ cup shortening
1 cup sour cream   2 eggs
          1 teasp. vanilla

Be sure that all ingredients are at room temperature. Combine melted chocolate and boiling water, stirring until well blended. Sift flour, soda, salt, and sugar together. Add shortening and sour cream (if you don't have sour cream, add 1 Tbsp. lemon juice to 1 cup sweet cream) Beat for 2 minutes. Add cooled chocolate mixture and unbeaten egg. Put batter into 2 greased and floured 8 inch layer cake pans. Bake in a moderate oven (350°F.) 35 to 40 minutes. If you use butter, margarine, or lard, decrease sour cream by 2 Tbsp.

Delicate Cake

3 cups flour   2 cups sugar
2 eggs   1 teacup sweet milk
½ teacup butter   2 teasp. baking powder
          2 teasp. vanilla

Cream the butter and add the sugar gradually, then the eggs. Sift the flour and the baking powder together and add to the sugar mixture alternately with the milk. Bake in a sheet for 30 minutes (350°F)

Gypsy Cake

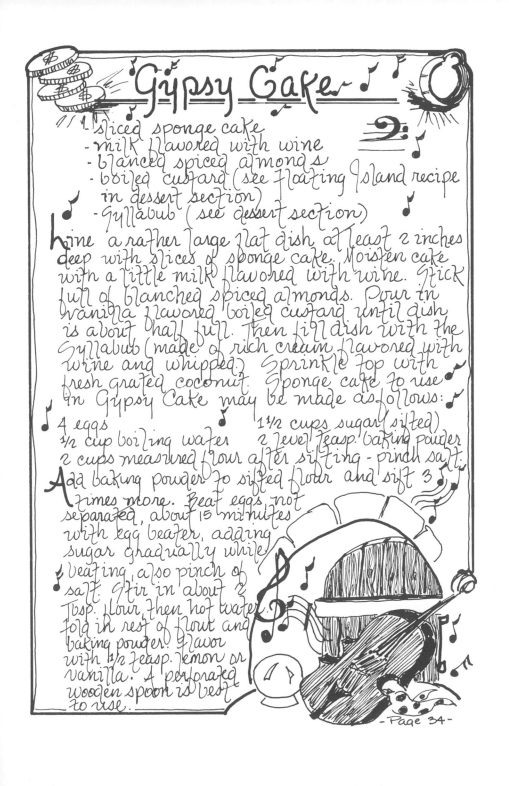

- sliced sponge cake
- milk flavored with wine
- blanched spiced almonds
- boiled custard (see Floating Island recipe in dessert section)
- Syllabub (see dessert section)

Line a rather large flat dish at least 2 inches deep with slices of sponge cake. Moisten cake with a little milk flavored with wine. Stick full of blanched spiced almonds. Pour in vanilla flavored boiled custard until dish is about half full. Then fill dish with the Syllabub (made of rich cream flavored with wine and whipped) Sprinkle top with fresh grated coconut. Sponge cake to use in Gypsy Cake may be made as follows:

4 eggs   1½ cups sugar (sifted)
½ cup boiling water   2 level teasp. baking powder
2 cups measured flour after sifting - pinch salt.

Add baking powder to sifted flour and sift 3 times more. Beat eggs, not separated, about 15 minutes with egg beater, adding sugar gradually while beating, also pinch of salt. Stir in about 2 Tbsp. flour, then hot water, fold in rest of flour and baking powder. Flavor with 1½ teasp. lemon or vanilla. A perforated wooden spoon is best to use.

Cup Cakes

½ cup shortening   1 cup sugar
3 eggs   1¾ cup flour
2 teasp. baking powder   ½ teasp. salt
½ cup milk   1 teasp. vanilla

Cream shortening and sugar. Add beaten eggs and mix well. Mix and sift flour, baking powder, and salt and add alternately with milk to the first mixture. Add vanilla and beat thoroughly. Pour into greased muffin tins and then bake in quick oven (425°F) 15 to 20 minutes. This recipe makes 15 to 20 cakes.

My Favorite Cake Recipe

1 cup shortening   2 cups sugar
1 cup milk   4 eggs
1 tedsp. vanilla   3 cups flour (1½ cups
plain flour + 1½ cups self-rising flour --- or
if all plain flour is used, add 4 teasp. baking
powder & ¾ teasp. salt.)

Add sugar gradually, creaming into shortening thoroughly. Add egg yolks one at a time and beat well. Add vanilla. Sift dry ingredients together & add alternately with milk. Beat egg whites stiff & fold into batter. Bake at (350°F). Yields 6 layers.

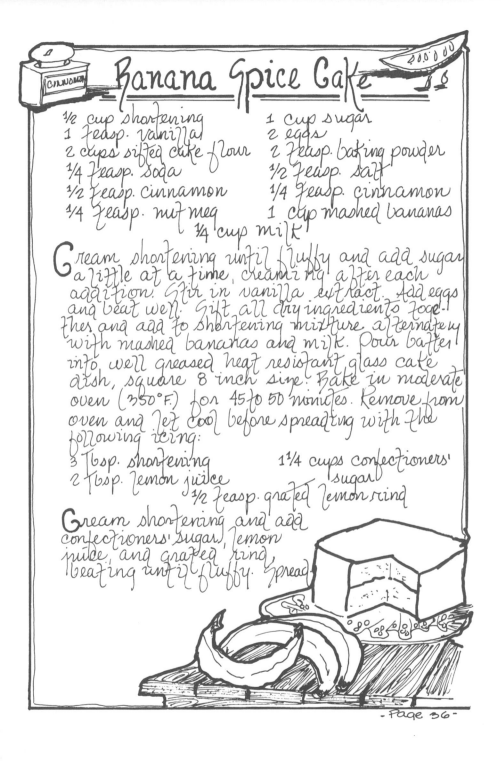

Banana Spice Cake

½ cup shortening	1 cup sugar
1 teasp. vanilla	2 eggs
2 cups sifted cake flour	2 teasp. baking powder
¼ teasp. soda	½ teasp. salt
½ teasp. cinnamon	¼ teasp. cinnamon
¼ teasp. nutmeg	1 cup mashed bananas

¼ cup milk

Cream shortening until fluffy and add sugar a little at a time, creaming after each addition. Stir in vanilla extract. Add eggs and beat well. Sift all dry ingredients together and add to shortening mixture alternately with mashed bananas and milk. Pour batter into well greased heat resistant glass cake dish, square 8 inch size. Bake in moderate oven (350°F.) for 45 to 50 minutes. Remove from oven and let cool before spreading with the following icing:

3 Tbsp. shortening	1¼ cups confectioners' sugar
2 Tbsp. lemon juice	

½ teasp. grated lemon rind

Cream shortening and add confectioners' sugar, lemon juice, and grated rind, beating until fluffy. Spread.

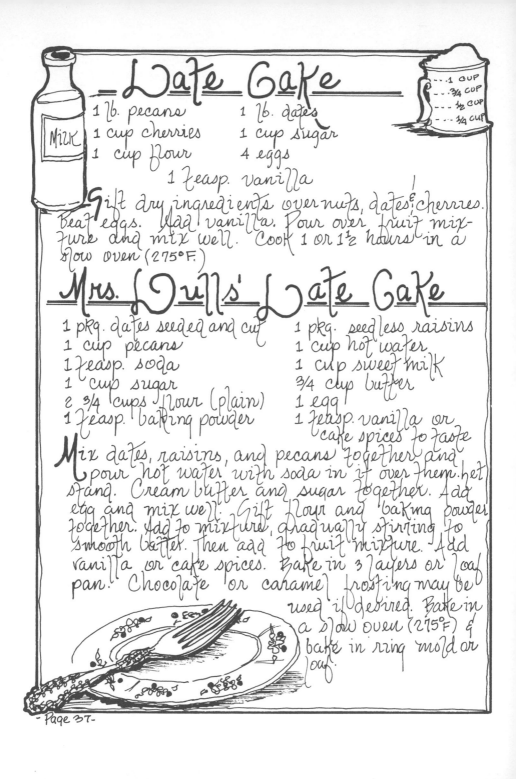

Date Cake

1 lb. pecans	1 lb. dates
1 cup cherries	1 cup sugar
1 cup flour	4 eggs

1 teasp. vanilla

Sift dry ingredients over nuts, dates & cherries. Beat eggs. Add vanilla. Pour over fruit mixture and mix well. Cook 1 or 1½ hours in a slow oven (275°F.)

Mrs. Dulls' Date Cake

1 pkg. dates seeded and cut	1 pkg. seedless raisins
1 cup pecans	1 cup hot water
1 teasp. soda	1 cup sweet milk
1 cup sugar	3/4 cup butter
2 3/4 cups flour (plain)	1 egg
1 teasp. baking powder	1 teasp. vanilla or cake spices to taste

Mix dates, raisins, and pecans together and pour hot water with soda in it over them. Let stand. Cream butter and sugar together. Add egg and mix well. Sift flour and baking powder together. Add to mixture, gradually stirring to smooth batter. Then add to fruit mixture. Add vanilla or cake spices. Bake in 3 layers or loaf pan. Chocolate or caramel frosting may be used if desired. Bake in a slow oven (275°F) & bake in ring mold or loaf.

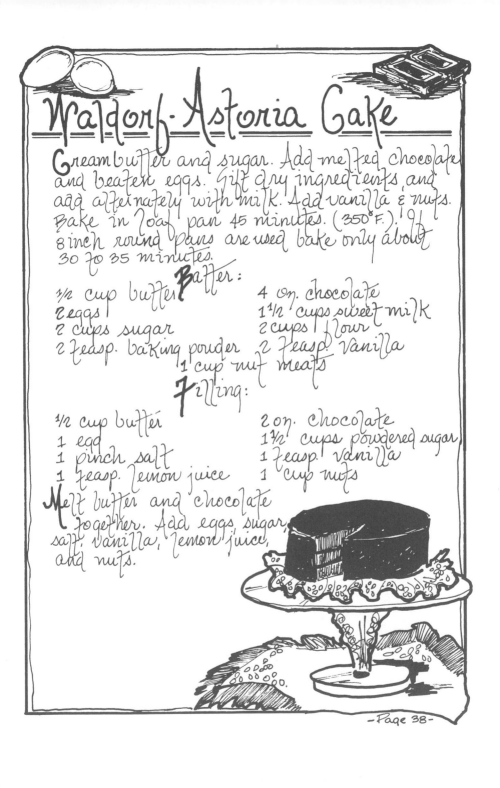

Waldorf-Astoria Cake

Cream butter and sugar. Add melted chocolate and beaten eggs. Sift dry ingredients, and add alternately with milk. Add vanilla & nuts. Bake in loaf pan 45 minutes. (350°F.). If 8 inch round pans are used bake only about 30 to 35 minutes.

Batter:

½ cup butter	4 oz. chocolate
2 eggs	1½ cups sweet milk
2 cups sugar	2 cups flour
2 teasp. baking powder	2 teasp. vanilla
1 cup nut meats	

Filling:

½ cup butter	2 oz. chocolate
1 egg	1½ cups powdered sugar
1 pinch salt	1 teasp. vanilla
1 teasp. lemon juice	1 cup nuts

Melt butter and chocolate together. Add eggs, sugar, salt, vanilla, lemon juice, and nuts.

Grandmas' Pound Cake 100 Years Ago

2 cups sugar (1 lb.)   4 cups flour (1 lb.)
2 cups butter (1 lb.)   10 eggs (1 lb.)

Beat the yolks and whites of eggs separately. Cream butter and cream the sugar into it. Add the egg yolks, mix well, and add the stiff egg whites; alternately with the flour. Lots beating of air into this mixture is the success of this cake. Put in the oven when you can bear your hand on the bottom. Gradually increase the oven heat to moderate. (350°F.) Bake 2 hours. (Make 2)

Old Fashioned Pound Cake

2 cups butter   2 cups granulated sugar
10 eggs   ¼ Teasp. grated nutmeg
4 scant cups pastry flour ½ Teasp. salt

Beat the butter and sugar until very light and creamy. Beat the egg yolks well and then add them. Sift the flour, salt, and nutmeg together juice and add to butter mixture a little at a time. Whip the whites of eggs till very stiff and fold them into the cake batter as gently as possible. Line cake pans with waxed paper. Fill two-thirds full with batter, & bake in a moderate oven about 1½ hours. (350°F)

1·2·3·4 Cake

1 cup shortening	4 teasp. baking powder
2 cups sugar	1 cup milk
3 cups flour	4 eggs
3/4 teasp. salt	1 teasp. vanilla

Add sugar gradually, creaming into shortening thoroughly. Add the egg yolks one at a time & beat well. Add vanilla. Sift dry ingredients together and add alternately with milk. Beat egg whites stiff and fold in batter. Turn into greased pans and bake at 350°F. Yeilds 6 layers.

Self-Rising Flour Cake (good)

1 cup butter or shortening	3 eggs
1½ cups sugar	3/4 cup milk or water
2½ cups flour	1 teasp. vanilla
	(or other flavorings)

Cream butter or shortening with ½ cup flour. Add sugar and cream one egg at a time. Add milk and then 2 cups of flour. Add flavorings. Let stand 20 minutes. Then stir again before baking. Bake in moderate oven until done. (350°)

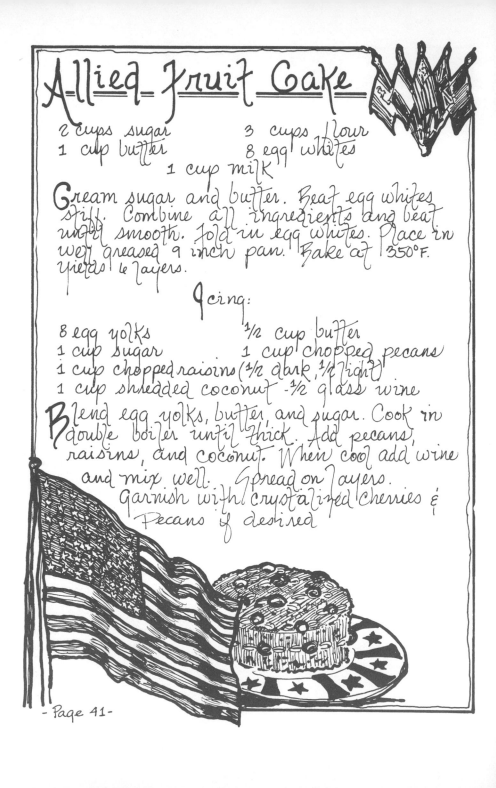

Allied Fruit Cake

2 cups sugar   3 cups flour
1 cup butter   8 egg whites
     1 cup milk

Cream sugar and butter. Beat egg whites stiff. Combine all ingredients and beat until smooth. Fold in egg whites. Place in well greased 9 inch pan. Bake at 350°F. Yields 6 layers.

Icing:

8 egg yolks   ½ cup butter
1 cup sugar   1 cup chopped pecans
1 cup chopped raisins (½ dark, ½ light)
1 cup shredded coconut - ½ glass wine

Blend egg yolks, butter, and sugar. Cook in double boiler until thick. Add pecans, raisins, and coconut. When cool add wine and mix well. Spread on layers.
Garnish with crystalized cherries & pecans if desired

White Fruit Cake

5 large eggs   ½ lb. butter
1 cup sugar   ¾ lb. crystallized cherries
1 lb. crystallized pineapple-4 cups nut meats
1 small bottle vanilla flavoring   (pecans)
1 small bottle lemon flavoring - 1¾ cups flour
½ teasp. baking powder

Cream butter and sugar. Add well beaten eggs.
Chop nuts and fruit (use whole if desired) and
mix with 1 cup flour. Sift remaining flour
and baking powder together. Add to butter
and egg mixture. Add fruit, nuts, and flavoring. Grease pans and line with brown
paper only on bottom. Grease paper. Put in
cold oven and bake for about 30 minutes
at 300°F, then at 250 degrees for 2½ hours.
Makes about 5 pounds (2 sm. cakes - or 1 large)

Christmas Cakes

1 quart best New Orleans molasses
3/4 lb. brown sugar
3/4 lb. lard and butter mixed
2 heaped teasp. soda
1 oz. ginger - ½ cup boiling water
1 oz. cinnamon - 1 oz ground cloves
Enough flour to make a rather stiff dough.

1. Mix molasses, lard and butter after having first warmed them in separate vessels to a luke warm temperature.

2. Add the sugar, beating the mixture all the time.

3. Put soda into half cup of boiling water, stir and add this to the above mixture.

4. Mix the ginger, cinnamon, and cloves with some of the flour and stir into mixture.

5. Add the rest of flour to make a dough about the consistancy of bread dough.

6. Let this dough stand in a cool place for at least twenty-four hours to season before beginning to bake your cakes. Bake in moderate oven (250°F.) Ice as desired. 40 to 60 minutes

Japanese Fruit Cake

1 cup butter   1 teasp. allspice
2 cups sugar   1 teasp. cinnamon
3¼ cups flour   ½ teasp. cloves
4 eggs   (ground)
1 cup water or milk ¼ lb. raisins (light
2 teasp. baking powder   & dark)
       1 teasp. vanilla
¼ cup cocoa (for 2 layers)

Cream butter and sugar. Add well
beaten eggs. Mix 3 cups flour with
baking powder. Add to butter mixture alternating with milk (or
water). Add vanilla. Beat mixture thoroughly until smooth.
Divide batter into two
parts. Add cocoa to one bowl and
mix well. To the second bowl add
allspice, cinnamon, & cloves, mix
well. Dust raisins with the
remaining ¼ cup flour and
fold into second bowl.
Bake both parts
into two layers
each. Filling:
juice of 2 lemons
grated rind of 1 lemon
1 good sized coconut grated
2 cups sugar
1 cup boiling water
2 Tbsp. cornstarch dis-
solved in ½ cup water.
Mix ingredients and cook, stirring constantly until mixture drops in a lump from the spoon.
Cool and spread between layers of cake. Cover top with
white butter icing and sprinkle with coconut.

Fruit Cake

1 lb. butter
1 lb. sugar
1 lb. eggs (9 or 10)
1 lb. plain flour
1 teasp. cream of tartar
1 teasp. allspice
1 teasp. nutmeg
1 teasp. ginger
1 teasp. ground cloves
1 lb. brown sugar

1 wineglass of wine
2 lbs. raisins
2 lbs currants or raisins
1/2 lb. citron (or water melon preserves drained)
1 lb. crystalized pineapple
1/2 lb. crystalized cherries
1 lemon peel
1 orange peel
1 teasp. vanilla

Cream butter and sugar together. Beat in eggs & add wine. Combine the spices, vanilla & flour. Mix with fruit, then add to first mixture, mixing all ingredients thoroughly. Put in a greased pan with brown paper on the bottom. Bake in a slow oven (250°F) for 3 hours

Delicious Loaf or Layer Cake

3/4 cup of butter or shortening
3 eggs
3/4 cup milk or water

1 1/2 cups sugar
2 1/2 cups self-rising flour
1 teasp. lemon flavoring

Cream the butter with 1/2 cup flour. Add the sugar, then one egg at a time, creaming mixture well. Add two cups flour and lemon flavoring. Let set for 20 minutes and stir until smooth. Bake in 4 layers. (350°F.) 30 to 40 minutes. Measure all ingredients in a large cup.

Soft Molasses Cake

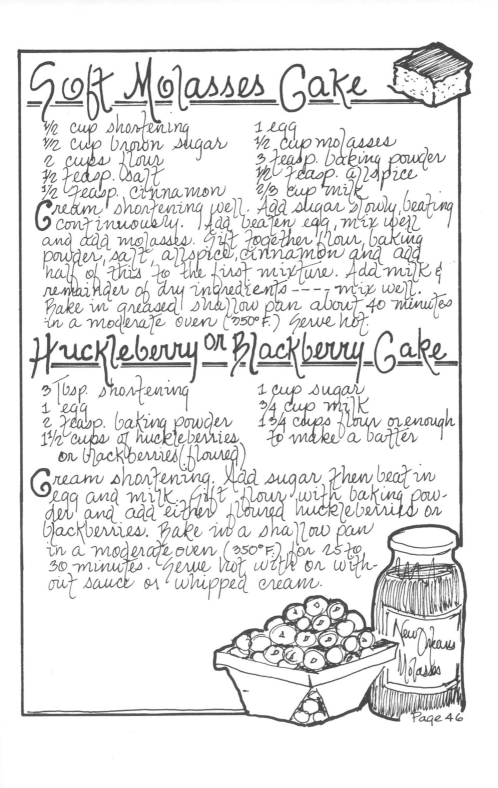

½ cup shortening
½ cup brown sugar
2 cups flour
½ teasp. salt
½ teasp. cinnamon

1 egg
½ cup molasses
3 teasp. baking powder
½ teasp. allspice
2/3 cup milk

Cream shortening well. Add sugar slowly, beating continuously. Add beaten egg, mix well and add molasses. Sift together flour, baking powder, salt, allspice, cinnamon and add half of this to the first mixture. Add milk & remainder of dry ingredients --- mix well. Bake in greased shallow pan about 40 minutes in a moderate oven (350° F.) Serve hot.

Huckleberry OR Blackberry Cake

3 Tbsp. shortening
1 egg
2 teasp. baking powder
1½ cups of huckleberries
  or blackberries (floured)

1 cup sugar
¾ cup milk
1¾ cups flour or enough
to make a batter

Cream shortening. Add sugar then beat in egg and milk. Sift flour with baking powder and add either floured huckleberries or blackberries. Bake in a shallow pan in a moderate oven (350° F.) for 25 to 30 minutes. Serve hot with or without sauce or whipped cream.

New Orleans Molasses

Angel Food Cake

1 cup of sifted plain cake flour
1 cup of egg whites (8-10) eggs
1/4 Teasp. salt   1 Teasp. cream of tartar
3/4 Teasp. vanilla   1/4 Teasp. almond extract
1 1/4 cups sifted granulated sugar

Sift flour once, measure and sift four more times. Beat egg whites and salt. When foamy add cream of tartar and continue beating until eggs are stiff enough to hold up in peaks, but not dry. Fold in sugar carefully, two tablespoons at a time until all is used. Fold in flavoring. Then sift small quantity of flour over mixture. Fold in carefully. Continue until all is used. Pour batter into ungreased angel food pan and bake at least one hour in a slow oven. (275°F.). Begin at 275°F. and after 30 minutes increase heat to 325°F. and bake 30 minutes longer. Remove from oven and invert pan for 1 hour (or until cold.

Devil Food Cake

1 small cake of chocolate   1 egg
1 cup brown sugar   ½ cup milk

Blend above ingredients and cook until it thickens. Set to cool before going on to 2nd step.

1 cup butter   1 cup brown sugar
½ cup milk   2½ cups flour
2 eggs   1 Teasp. soda
1 Teasp. vanilla   few drops of almond extract

Mix as usual cake. Cream butter and sugar. Add eggs one at a time, then flour and soda and milk, stirring smooth. Add first mixture and flavor with vanilla and a few drops of almond extract. Bake in layers and put together with following filling when layers are cool.

Marshmallow Icing

1½ cups sugar   ½ cup water
3 egg whites beaten stiff   6 marshmallows chopped
            ¼ Teaspoon salt

Mix sugar and water and cook until it forms a thread when dropped from spoon. Pour hot mixture over stiff egg whites & beat well. Add 6 marshmallows and salt. Beat until holds shape. Spread.

Coconut Cake

1 cup butter   2 cups sugar
3½ cups flour   5 eggs
3 teasp. baking powder   1 cup milk
                1 teasp. vanilla

Mix as for any layer cake and beat until very smooth. Bake at 350°F for 35 to 40 minutes.

Icing:

3 egg whites beaten to a stiff froth
2 cups sugar   ½ cup water
2 light cups grated coconut
1 teaspoon vanilla   ¼ teaspoon lemon extract

Boil sugar and water till it threads when dropped from a fork. Take from fire and pour very slowly over the whites of eggs, beating very fast. Add coconut, then flavorings. Stir until cool. Spread between layers of cake and over the top and sides.

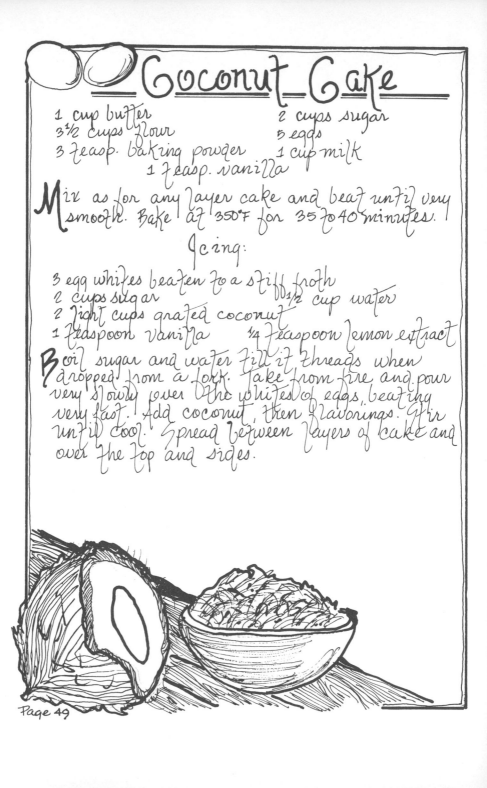

Caramel Pecan Layer Cake

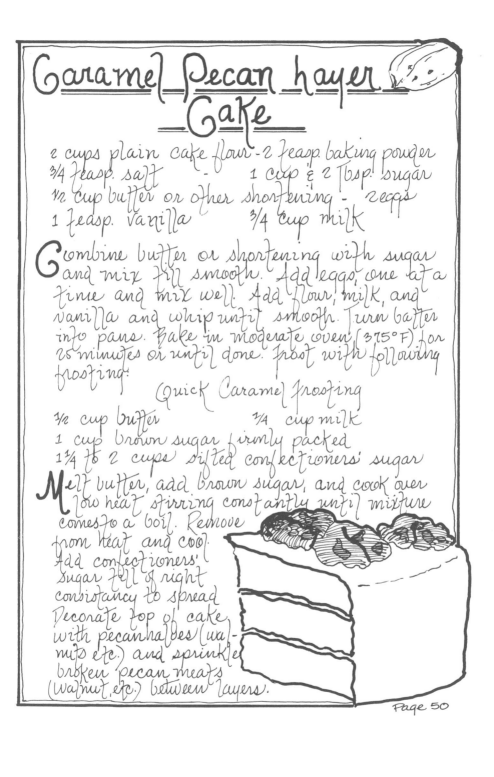

2 cups plain cake flour - 2 teasp. baking powder
3/4 teasp. salt - 1 cup & 2 Tbsp. sugar
1/2 cup butter or other shortening - 2 eggs
1 teasp. vanilla   3/4 cup milk

Combine butter or shortening with sugar
and mix till smooth. Add eggs, one at a
time and mix well. Add flour, milk, and
vanilla and whip until smooth. Turn batter
into pans. Bake in moderate oven (375°F) for
25 minutes or until done. Frost with following
frosting:

Quick Caramel Frosting

1/2 cup butter   3/4 cup milk
1 cup brown sugar firmly packed
1 1/4 to 2 cups sifted confectioners' sugar

Melt butter, add brown sugar, and cook over
low heat stirring constantly until mixture
comes to a boil. Remove
from heat and cool.
Add confectioners'
sugar till of right
consistancy to spread
Decorate top of cake
with pecan halves (wal-
nuts etc.) and sprinkle
broken pecan meats
(walnut etc.) between layers.

Hot Milk Cake

4 eggs   2 cups sugar
1 cup milk   ¼ lb. butter
2 cups plain flour   1 teasp. baking powder

Break eggs into large bowl and beat with a dover egg beater. Add sugar. Put milk and butter on stove and heat until butter melts. Sift flour and baking powder together and add to egg mixture. Combine well. Add hot milk and butter, mix well and pour immediately into well greased and floured cake tins while batter is still hot and bake about 20 minutes in an oven hot enough to bake biscuits. (425°F.). Turn out immediately upon cake rack to cool and cut in half for 2 layers. (Try baking this sometime in a tube cake pan at 375°F for about an hour. Nice for the Kiddies' birthday.)

This is my favorite layer cake recipe and with it I use chocolate, coconut, or caramel icing. It makes delicious party cakes when cut into 2 inch squares, iced and decorated. (One time I cut them with a heart cookie cutter, iced them white and wrote my guests' names with red icing for a valentine party.

Rusk

½ yeast cake   1 cup tepid water
1 cup sugar   ½ cup butter
2 well beaten eggs   ¾ cup cold water
      flour as called for

Let yeast cake soak in the tepid water a few minutes until dissolved. Stir well and pour into bowl. Add ¾ cup cold water. Stir. Sift enough plain flour into this to make a stiff batter. Set to rise overnight. Next morning, stir down and add sugar, well beaten eggs and butter to batter. (raised dough) Sift with enough flour to make dough in a large wooden mixing bowl. Knead well, working in flour enough to make a good bread dough. The butter is worked in as the dough is kneaded. Set to rise until dough is light. Then make into high biscuits. Set closely in the pan. Let rise again. When raised, they should be about 3 inches high. Brush with drawn butter, sift a little sugar and cinnamon on top and bake in a moderate oven (350°F)

Pineapple Upside-Down Cake

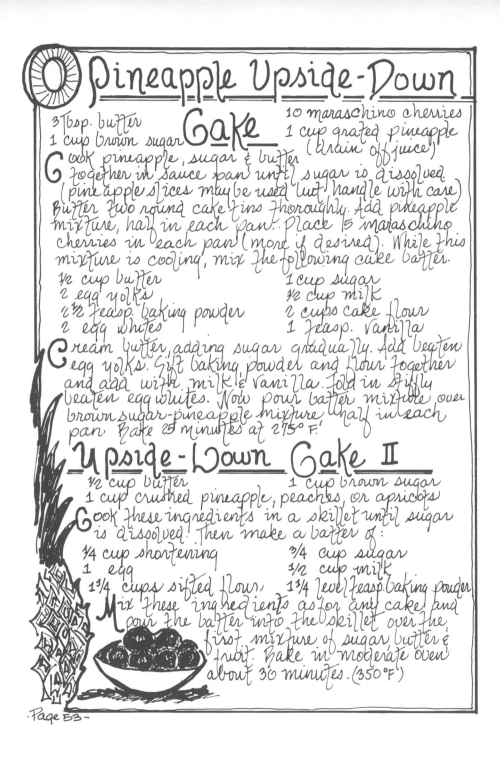

3 Tbsp. butter
1 cup brown sugar

10 maraschino cherries
1 cup grated pineapple (drain off juice)

Cook pineapple, sugar & butter together in sauce pan until sugar is dissolved (pineapple slices may be used but handle with care) Butter two round cake tins thoroughly. Add pineapple mixture, half in each pan. Place 5 maraschino cherries in each pan (more if desired). While this mixture is cooling, mix the following cake batter.

½ cup butter
2 egg yolks
1½ teasp. baking powder
2 egg whites

1 cup sugar
½ cup milk
2 cups cake flour
1 teasp. vanilla

Cream butter, adding sugar gradually. Add beaten egg yolks. Sift baking powder and flour together and add with milk & vanilla. Fold in stiffly beaten egg whites. Now pour batter mixture over brown sugar-pineapple mixture half in each pan. Bake 25 minutes at 275° F.

Upside-Down Cake II

½ cup butter
1 cup crushed pineapple, peaches, or apricots

1 cup brown sugar

Cook these ingredients in a skillet until sugar is dissolved. Then make a batter of:

¼ cup shortening
1 egg
1¼ cups sifted flour

¾ cup sugar
½ cup milk
1¾ level teasp. baking powder

Mix these ingredients as for any cake and pour the batter into the skillet over the first mixture of sugar, butter & fruit. Bake in moderate oven about 30 minutes. (350°F)

Toasted Spice Cake

⅓ cup butter   1 cup sugar
2 egg yolks   ½ teasp. soda
⅔ cup buttermilk   1¼ cups plain flour
½ teasp. cinnamon   ½ teasp. cake spice
½ teasp. salt   ½ teasp. vanilla

Cream butter, sugar, and egg yolks. Dissolve soda in buttermilk. Sift together flour, baking powder, cinnamon, cake spice and salt. Combine buttermilk mixture and flour mixture alternately into sugar mixture. Add vanilla and blend well. Pour into shallow pan (8 in. or 12 in.) which has been well greased & floured.

Brown Sugar Meringue

2 egg whites   ½ cup brown sugar
nut meats (as many as desired)

Beat egg whites until they hold a point, but not dry. Add sugar slowly and continue beating until smooth. Spread meringue on raw cake batter and sprinkle with broken nut meats. Bake in a moderate oven (350°F) for 35 or 40 minutes. Cut in squares and serve hot or cold.

Sponge Cake

2 eggs well beaten   1 cup sugar.
1 cup sifted flour   1 teasp. baking powder
½ cup sweet milk   1 Tbsp. butter
1 pinch salt   1 teasp. vanilla

Add butter to milk and let come to boiling point but do not boil. Mix eggs, sugar, flour, baking powder, salt and vanilla, and beat well. Add milk and butter. Bake at 350°F. 20 to 30 minutes. Take cake out and let cool for several minutes. Then spread top with the following icing:

1 cup brown sugar   3 Tbsp. sweet milk
½ cup crushed nuts   1 cup pineapple

Mix ingredients and spead over cake. Put back in oven (or under broiler) until brown. Delicious.

Busy Day Cake

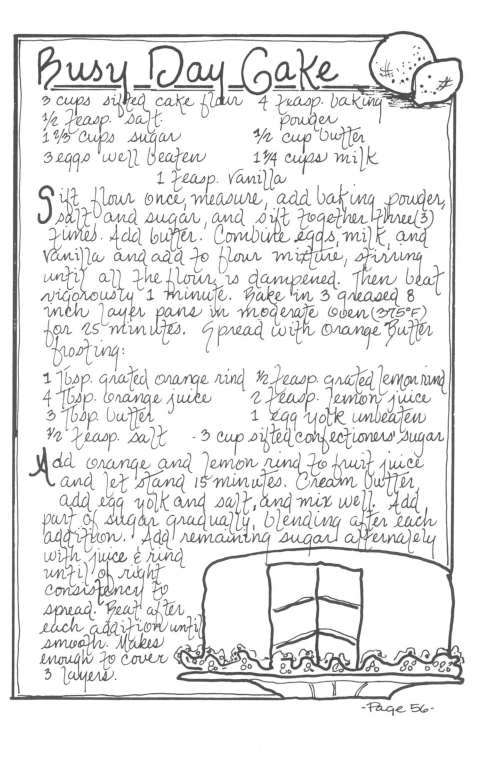

3 cups sifted cake flour   4 teasp. baking
½ teasp. salt   powder
1 ⅔ cups sugar   ½ cup butter
3 eggs well beaten   1¼ cups milk
1 teasp. vanilla

Sift flour once, measure, add baking powder,
salt and sugar, and sift together three (3)
times. Add butter. Combine eggs, milk, and
vanilla and add to flour mixture, stirring
until all the flour is dampened. Then beat
vigorously 1 minute. Bake in 3 greased 8
inch layer pans in moderate oven (375°F)
for 25 minutes. Spread with Orange Butter
frosting:

1 Tbsp. grated orange rind ½ teasp. grated lemon rind
4 Tbsp. orange juice   2 teasp. lemon juice
3 Tbsp. butter   1 egg yolk unbeaten
½ teasp. salt   ·3 cup sifted confectioners' sugar

Add orange and lemon rind to fruit juice
and let stand 15 minutes. Cream butter,
add egg yolk and salt, and mix well. Add
part of sugar gradually, blending after each
addition. Add remaining sugar alternately
with juice & rind
until of right
consistency to
spread. Beat after
each addition until
smooth. Makes
enough to cover
3 layers.

Two Egg Cake

2 cups sifted cake flour   1⅓ cups sugar
2½ teasp. double acting baking powder
1 teasp. salt   ½ cup shortening
⅞ cup of milk   1¼ teasp. vanilla
                2 eggs

Sift flour, sugar, baking powder, and salt into small mixing bowl. Add shortening, two-thirds of milk and vanilla. Beat at least 2 minutes. Add eggs and remaining milk. Beat 2 minutes more. Pour into two greased deep 8 inch cake tins. Bake in oven at 350° for 30 to 35 minutes. Frost with your favorite frosting.

No Egg Cake

1 cup and two tablespoons sugar
¼ cup butter   2 cups flour
1 teasp. vanilla   ½ cup milk

Mix as any other cake. Makes 2 layers.

Filling
2 cups confectioners sugar.   1 Tbsp. butter
1 Tbsp. sweet cream   ½ cup of breakfast cocoa

Mix sugar, butter & cream. Mix well to good consistency for spreading. Add the breakfast cocoa, mix well. Spread.

One Egg Cake

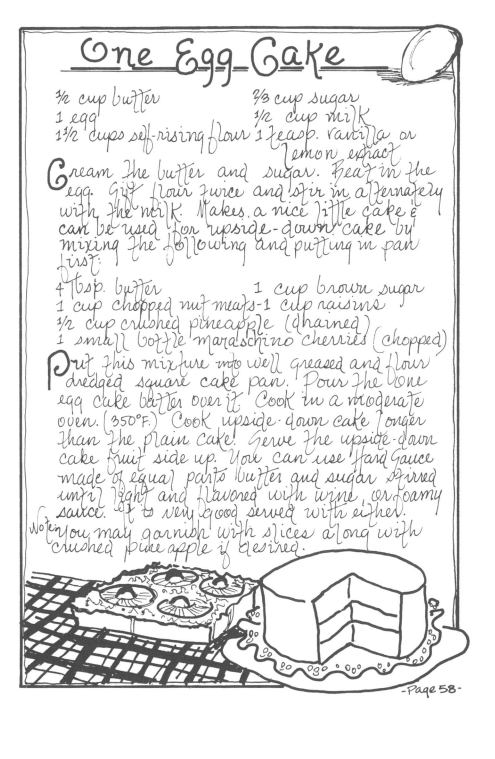

½ cup butter
1 egg
1½ cups self-rising flour

⅔ cup sugar
½ cup milk
1 teasp. vanilla or lemon extract

Cream the butter and sugar. Beat in the egg. Sift flour twice and stir in alternately with the milk. Makes a nice little cake & can be used for upside-down cake by mixing the following and putting in pan first:

4 Tbsp. butter   1 cup brown sugar
1 cup chopped nut meats—1 cup raisins
½ cup crushed pineapple (drained)
1 small bottle maraschino cherries (chopped)

Put this mixture into well greased and flour dredged square cake pan. Pour the One egg cake batter over it. Cook in a moderate oven. (350°F.) Cook upside-down cake longer than the plain cake. Serve the upside-down cake fruit side up. You can use Hard Sauce made of equal parts butter and sugar stirred until light and flavored with wine, or foamy sauce. It is very good served with either.

Note: You may garnish with slices along with crushed pineapple if desired.

Honey Icing

½ cup strained honey
1 Tbsp. syrup
1 egg white

With the water boiling vigorously in a double boiler, place the above ingredients in the upper part and beat constantly with a dover beater for several minutes. Spread while warm, finishing the surface smoothly with a buttered knife to prevent sticking

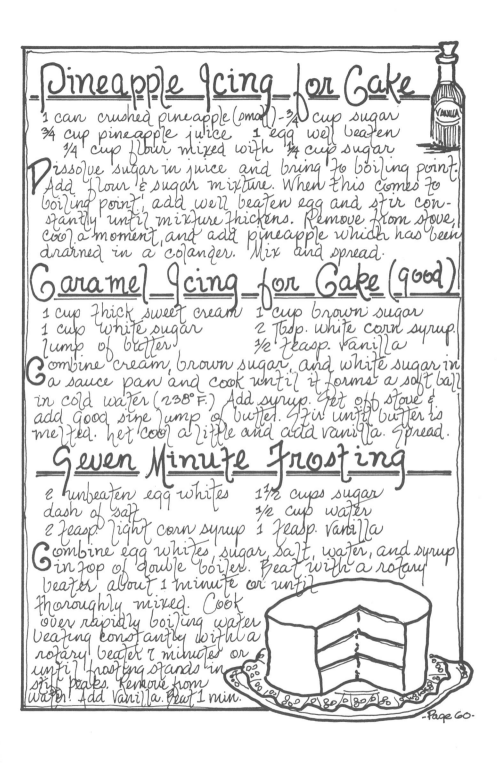

Pineapple Icing for Cake

1 can crushed pineapple (small) - ¾ cup sugar
¾ cup pineapple juice   1 egg well beaten
   ¼ cup flour mixed with ¼ cup sugar

Dissolve sugar in juice and bring to boiling point.
Add flour & sugar mixture. When this comes to
boiling point, add well beaten egg and stir constantly until mixture thickens. Remove from stove,
cool a moment, and add pineapple which has been
drained in a colander. Mix and spread.

Caramel Icing for Cake (good)

1 cup thick sweet cream   1 cup brown sugar
1 cup white sugar   2 Tbsp. white corn syrup.
lump of butter   ½ teasp. vanilla

Combine cream, brown sugar, and white sugar in
a sauce pan and cook until it forms a soft ball
in cold water (238°F.) Add syrup. Get off stove &
add good size lump of butter. Stir until butter is
melted. Let cool a little and add vanilla. Spread.

Seven Minute Frosting

2 unbeaten egg whites   1½ cups sugar
dash of salt   ½ cup water
2 teasp. light corn syrup 1 teasp. vanilla

Combine egg whites, sugar, salt, water, and syrup
in top of double boiler. Beat with a rotary
beater about 1 minute or until
thoroughly mixed. Cook
over rapidly boiling water
beating constantly with a
rotary beater 7 minutes or
until frosting stands in
stiff peaks. Remove from
water. Add vanilla. Beat 1 min.

Plain Boiled Icing

1½ cups sugar   1 cup cold water
2 egg whites beaten stiff.
Boil sugar & water together until it forms a hard ball when dropped in cold water. Have 2 egg whites beaten stiff and pour boiling sugar over them. Beat until cool enough to stand up on cake. If it gets too stiff and creamy, add a little hot water to thin. The success is in the beating. Spread

Lemon Icing for Cake (good)

1 coffee cup sugar (not quite a measuring cup)
2 Tbsp. butter   2 eggs (un separated)
juice of 2 lemons (rind if desired)
Beat all together and cook over boiling water until consistency of jelly. For orange icing substitute oranges for lemons. Double recipe for a large cake.

Chocolate Icing for Cake (good)

1½ cups sugar   ½ cup milk
½ cup cocoa   6 Tbsp. butter
Pinch salt   1 teasp. vanilla
Boil 1½ min-   utes &   beat a little.
Add vanilla   Spread   as it cools.
Delicious.

Soft Molasses Cookies

4½ cups all purpose flour - 1 Teasp. baking soda
1 Teasp. salt   3 Teasp. ginger
1 cup butter or shortening - 2 eggs
1 cup sifted brown sugar, firmly packed
¾ cup sour milk   ¾ cup molasses

Sift, then measure flour. Sift again with baking
soda, ginger, and salt. Cream butter. Add
sugar gradually and beat until light and
fluffy. Blend in well beaten eggs, then add
the molasses and continue to beat. Add dry
ingredients alternately with milk, beating
after each addition. Chill dough for several
hours. Turn onto floured board. Roll to ¼ inch
thickness. Cut with cookie   cutter or form
a roll of the dough 3 inches   in diameter
and cut slices   ¼ inch
thick. Sprinkle with
granulated
sugar.
Grease baking
sheets & bake
cookies in hot
oven. (450°F.)
This makes
3 dozen
3 inch
cookies

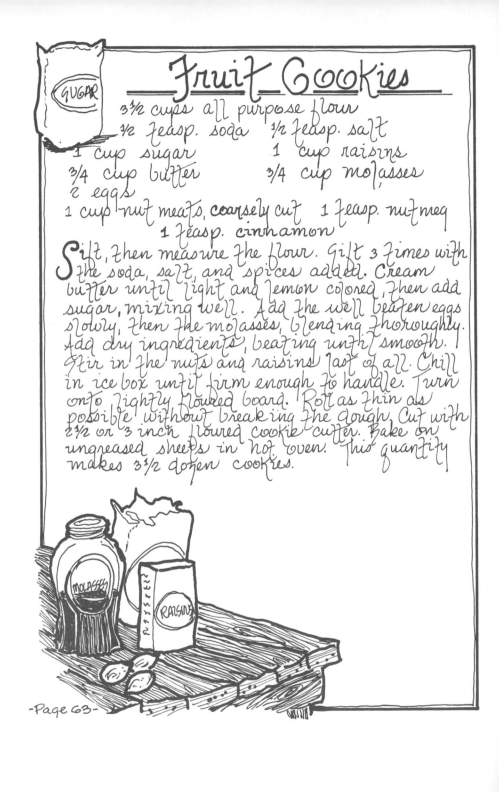

Fruit Cookies

3½ cups all purpose flour
½ teasp. soda   ½ teasp. salt
1 cup sugar   1 cup raisins
¾ cup butter   ¾ cup molasses
2 eggs
1 cup nut meats, coarsely cut   1 teasp. nutmeg
           1 teasp. cinnamon

Sift, then measure the flour. Sift 3 times with the soda, salt, and spices added. Cream butter until light and lemon colored, then add sugar, mixing well. Add the well beaten eggs slowly, then the molasses, blending thoroughly. Add dry ingredients, beating until smooth. Stir in the nuts and raisins last of all. Chill in ice box until firm enough to handle. Turn onto lightly floured board. Roll as thin as possible without breaking the dough. Cut with 2½ or 3 inch floured cookie cutter. Bake on ungreased sheets in hot oven. This quantity makes 3½ dozen cookies.

Confection Cookies

⅞ cup butter   4 Tbsp. powdered sugar
2 cups or more of pastry flour   1 teasp water
2 teasp. vanilla   1 cup chopped pecans

Cream butter and powdered sugar together. Add flour. Stir in water and vanilla. Add pecan meats. Mix thoroughly and place in ice box until cool enough to mold with fingers. Form pieces of dough into date-shaped forms. Place on baking sheet and bake in 400°F oven until light brown. When cool roll cookies in powdered sugar.

Butter Cookies

1½ sticks of butter   ½ cup sugar
2 egg yolks   2 cups flour

Cream butter and sugar together and add egg yolks. Then mix in flour. Pinch off pieces the size of marbles and roll in palm of hand, forming round balls. Place on ungreased cookie sheet. Make dent in each cookie with thumb and fill dent with apple jelly (or favorite jelly). Cook in 350°F oven 15 minutes.

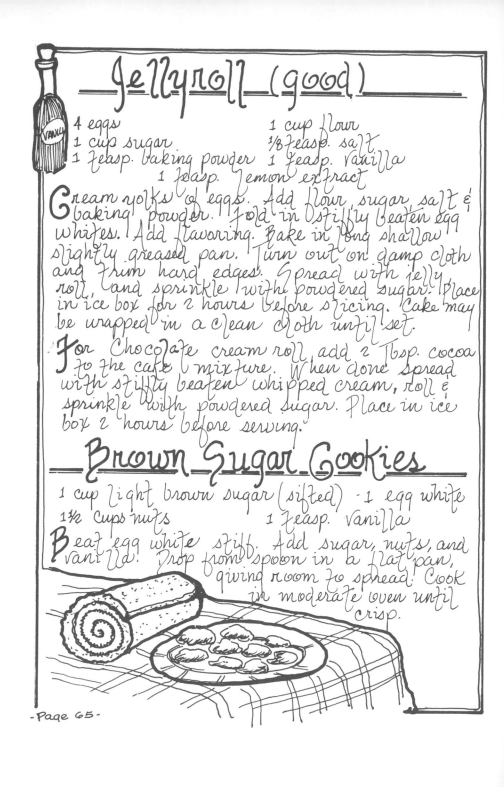

Jellyroll (good)

4 eggs   1 cup flour
1 cup sugar   1/8 teasp. salt
1 teasp. baking powder   1 teasp. vanilla
            1 teasp. lemon extract

Cream yolks of eggs. Add flour, sugar, salt & baking powder. Fold in stiffly beaten egg whites. Add flavoring. Bake in long shallow slightly greased pan. Turn out on damp cloth and trim hard edges. Spread with jelly roll, and sprinkle with powdered sugar. Place in ice box for 2 hours before slicing. Cake may be wrapped in a clean cloth until set.

For Chocolate cream roll, add 2 Tbsp. cocoa to the cake mixture. When done spread with stiffly beaten whipped cream, roll & sprinkle with powdered sugar. Place in ice box 2 hours before serving.

Brown Sugar Cookies

1 cup light brown sugar (sifted) · 1 egg white
1½ cups nuts   1 teasp. vanilla

Beat egg white stiff. Add sugar, nuts, and vanilla. Drop from spoon in a flat pan, giving room to spread. Cook in moderate oven until crisp.

Pastry Dates

1½ cups flour   ½ lb. cheese
¼ lb. butter   dates & nuts

Mix butter till creamy. Add grated cheese and cream well. Then mix in flour till it makes a firm dough. Roll out and cut with biscuit cutter. Wrap around date which has been stuffed with nut. Bake at 350°F about 15 or 20 minutes.

Butterscotch Squares

¼ cup butter   1 cup brown sugar
1 teasp. baking powder 1 egg
½ teasp. Vanilla   ¾ cup flour
        ¼ cup pecan meats

Cook butter and sugar together until smooth and well blended. Add egg and beat well. Add flour and baking powder, then vanilla and nuts. Spread in pan lined with paper. Bake in moderate oven (300°F.) for 30 minutes. Turn out of pan and cut in squares.

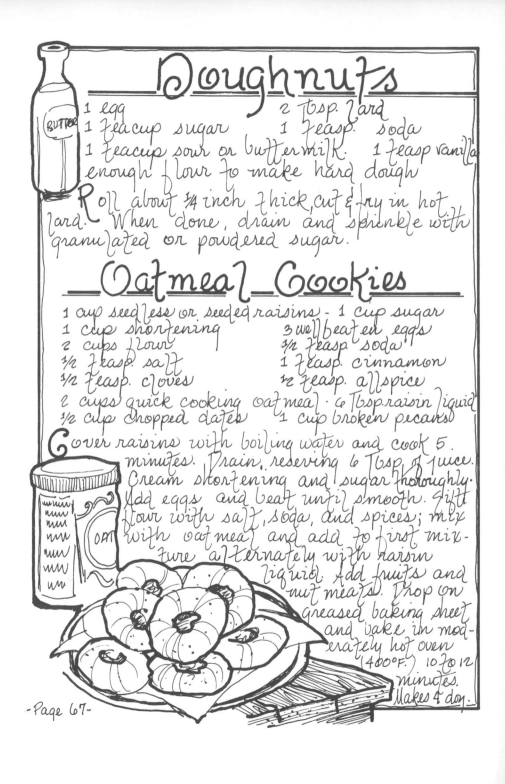

Doughnuts

1 egg	2 Tbsp. lard
1 teacup sugar	1 teasp. soda
1 teacup sour or buttermilk.	1 teasp vanilla

enough flour to make hard dough

Roll about ¼ inch thick, cut & fry in hot lard. When done, drain and sprinkle with granulated or powdered sugar.

Oatmeal Cookies

1 cup seedless or seeded raisins - 1 cup sugar
1 cup shortening   3 well beaten eggs
2 cups flour   ½ teasp. soda
½ teasp. salt   1 teasp. cinnamon
½ teasp. cloves   ½ teasp. allspice
2 cups quick cooking oatmeal - 6 Tbsp. raisin liquid
½ cup chopped dates   1 cup broken pecans

Cover raisins with boiling water and cook 5 minutes. Drain, reserving 6 Tbsp of juice. Cream shortening and sugar thoroughly. Add eggs and beat until smooth. Sift flour with salt, soda, and spices; mix with oatmeal and add to first mixture alternately with raisin liquid. Add fruits and nut meats. Drop on greased baking sheet and bake in moderately hot oven (400°F.) 10 to 12 minutes. Makes 4 doz.

Peanut Butter Cookies

½ cup peanut butter   ¼ cup shortening
½ cup brown sugar   ½ cup white
1 egg   sugar
1 cup flour   1 teasp. soda

Cream peanut butter and shortening together. Add sugar gradually and continue to
cream until mixture is light and fluffy. Add
egg. Sift flour and soda together. Add to other
mixture and mix thoroughly. Drop mixture
(level teaspoon at a time) on a cookie sheet.
Press down with fork tines and press second
time so that creases are at right angles.
Bake in moderate oven (350°F.) from 10 to 15
minutes. Makes 4½ dozen cookies.

Peanut Butter Pinwheels

½ cup shortening   ½ cup peanut butter
½ cup brown sugar
¼ cup corn syrup (dark)
1 egg (beaten)
1 cup sifted flour
½ teasp. salt

Cream shortening and pea-
nut butter together. Add
sugar & syrup, creaming until
thoroughly blended. Beat in
egg. Add flour & salt & stir
in well. Chill for 2 hours
Then shape in 1 inch balls.
Place balls on greased sheet
and press each flat with fork.
Bake in a moderate oven (375°F) for 10
minutes or until cookies are brown
Makes about 4 dozen cookies.

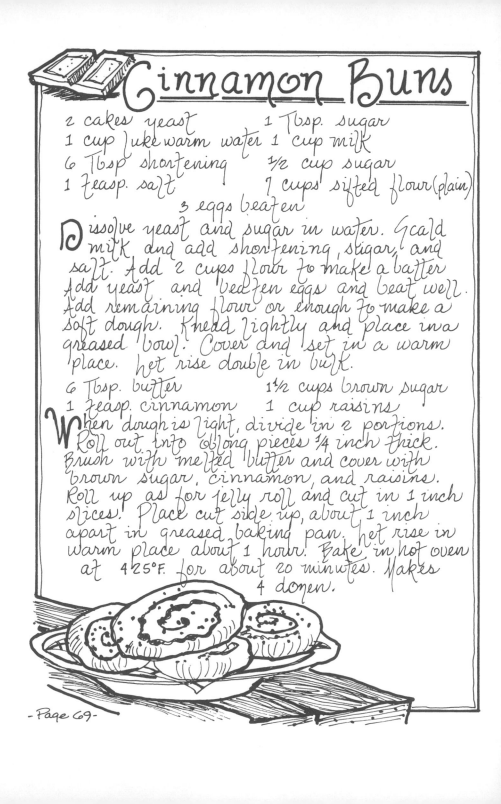

Cinnamon Buns

2 cakes yeast   1 Tbsp. sugar
1 cup luke warm water 1 cup milk
6 Tbsp shortening   ½ cup sugar
1 teasp. salt   7 cups sifted flour (plain)
              3 eggs beaten

Dissolve yeast and sugar in water. Scald milk and add shortening, sugar, and salt. Add 2 cups flour to make a batter. Add yeast and beaten eggs and beat well. Add remaining flour or enough to make a soft dough. Knead lightly and place in a greased bowl. Cover and set in a warm place. Let rise double in bulk.

6 Tbsp. butter   1½ cups brown sugar
1 teasp. cinnamon   1 cup raisins

When dough is light, divide in 2 portions. Roll out into oblong pieces ¼ inch thick. Brush with melted butter and cover with brown sugar, cinnamon, and raisins. Roll up as for jelly roll and cut in 1 inch slices. Place cut side up, about 1 inch apart in greased baking pan. Let rise in warm place about 1 hour. Bake in hot oven at 425°F. for about 20 minutes. Makes 4 dozen.

Cheese Thins

½ lb. butter   ½ lb. cheese
2 cups flour   pinch salt
Dash Tabasco, or red pepper

Cream butter, add grated cheese, and cream
well. Gradually add flour, salt, Tabasco
sauce or red pepper. Roll about ⅛ inch
thick, cut with cutter, decorate with pecan halves. Bake in moderate oven about
10 minutes. Dough will be easier to roll if you
let it stand in ice box for a while.

Ice Box Cheese Wafers

½ lb. grated strong cheese - ¼ lb. butter
½ teasp. salt   1¼ cups sifted flour
          Heavy pinch of cayenne

Cream cheese and butter, salt & pepper. Add
flour. Shape into sausage roll. Wrap in
waxed paper and keep in ice box as long
as desired. Slice thin and
bake in a moderate oven until
done.   A pecan half on each
          is decorative.

Ladyfingers

⅓ cup sifted all-purpose flour
⅛ teasp. salt   3 egg whites
2 egg yolks   ⅓ cup powdered sugar
          ½ teasp. vanilla

Heat oven to 350°F. Sift flour and salt together. Beat egg whites until stiff but not dry. Add powdered sugar gradually, continuing to beat until whites stand in peaks. Beat egg yolks until thick and lemon colored, then fold into egg whites. Add flour mixture and stir in vanilla. Using pastry bag with plain hole tube, shape dough into strips 1 inch wide and 4½ inches long, placed 2 inches apart on ungreased cookie sheet covered with plain or parchment paper. Sprinkle with powdered sugar. Bake in moderate oven of 350°F. for 12 minutes or until lightly browned. Cool slightly. Remove from paper with spatula. Cool on a wire rack. Makes about 20.

Peanut Cake Cookies

4 cups parched peanuts · 4 or 5 egg whites
          4 cups sugar

Add sugar to egg whites gradually. Eggs must be beaten stiff. Add ground up peanuts to mixture May drop by spoonfuls on greased cookie sheets. or bake in square pans Cook in about a 400°F. oven. until done

Nut Wafers

¼ cup lard
1 cup brown sugar
1¼ cups flour
½ teasp. lemon extract
½ teasp. vanilla

½ cup butter
1 egg beaten
¼ teasp. salt
½ teasp. soda
½ cup chopped nuts

Cream butter, lard, and sugar together. Add eggs. Sift dry ingredients and add to first mixture. Fold in nut meats and vanilla. Shape into roll, wrap in waxed paper, and store in ice box until needed. Slice and bake in a 400°F. oven for 7 to 12 minutes

Almond or Pecan Cookies

½ lb. shelled almonds or pecans
3 egg whites
½ teasp. cinnamon

1 cup white sugar
1 teasp. grated lemon rind

Dry nuts and put through a food chopper, using finest blade. Beat egg whites stiff. Fold in ground nuts, sugar, cinnamon, and lemon rind. Drop from a teaspoon onto a greased baking sheet. Bake in a slow oven (300°F.) for 15 minutes. Cool and store in a tightly covered container. These cookies will keep a long time & will improve in flavor. Makes about 400 small cookies.

Chocolate Bits Cookies

½ cup shortening   ¼ cup granulated sugar
½ cup brown sugar, firmly packed
½ teasp. vanilla   1 egg, well beaten
1 cup + 2 level Tbsp. sifted cake flour
½ teasp. soda   ½ teasp. salt
½ cup chopped nuts   1 pkg. chocolate bits

Cream shortening, both sugars, and vanilla until light and fluffy. Add egg and beat. Sift flour, soda, & salt together & add to first mixture.
Stir in nuts and chocolate bits. Mix thoroughly.
Drop from teaspoon on lightly greased cookie sheet. Bake in a moderately hot oven (375°F.) until done.

Pecan Patties

½ cup butter   1 cup brown sugar
½ cup white sugar   1 egg
½ cup flour   ¼ teasp. salt
2 cups chopped pecans

Cream butter. Add sugars gradually. Add well beaten egg yolk. Fold in stiffly beaten egg white. Add sifted flour & salt. Stir in pecans. Drop by spoon on well greased cookie sheet.
Bake at 350°F for 15 to 20 minutes.

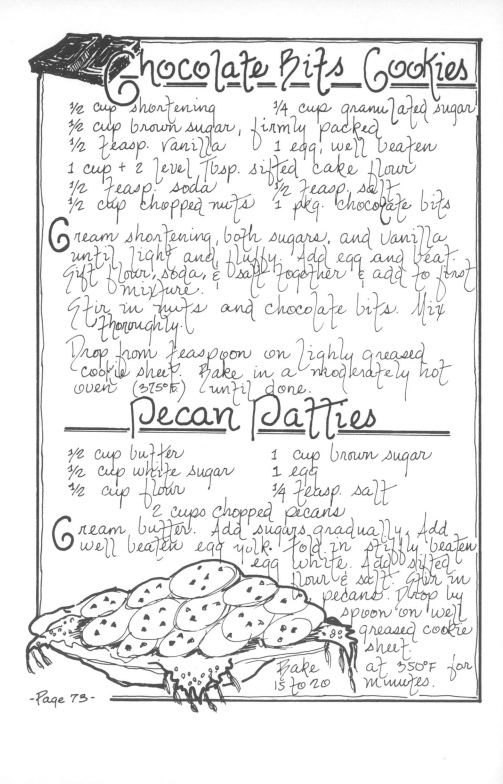

Brownies

¾ cup sifted cake flour   ¼ teasp. baking powder
¼ teasp. salt   ½ cup shortening
1 cup granulated sugar   2 eggs beaten
2 squares (2 oz.) unsweetened chocolate melted
¾ cup of chopped nuts or seeded raisins

Heat oven to 350°F. Sift flour, baking powder,
and salt together. Work shortening with spoon
until fluffy and creamy, then add sugar slowly
while continuing to work until light. Add
eggs and melted chocolate. Stir in flour
mixture with nuts. Turn into greased pan
8" x 8" x 2". Bake in a moderate oven (350°F.) for 30
to 35 minutes or until done. Immediately
cut into 2 inch squares with knife.
Sprinkle with powdered sugar. Cool.
Then remove from pan.

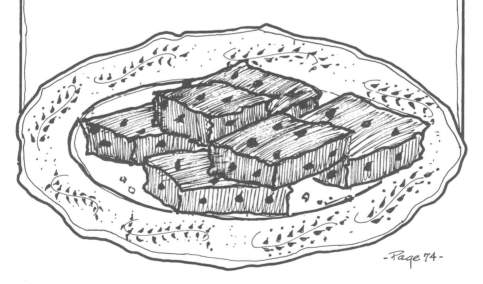

Pecan Crispies

½ cup shortening   ½ cup butter
2½ cups brown sugar   2 well beaten eggs
2½ cups flour   ¼ teasp. salt
½ teasp. soda   1 cup chopped pecan
             meats.

Cream shortening and sugar thoroughly. Add eggs and beat well. Add sifted dry ingredients then nut meats. Drop from teaspoon about 2 inches apart into greased cookie sheet. Bake in moderate oven (350°F.) 12 to 15 minutes. Makes 5 dozen

All-Bran Date Bars

3 eggs   ¾ teasp. baking powder
½ cup dates (cut fine)   1½ cups brown sugar
½ cup all-bran   ¾ cup flour
       1 cup nut meats (chopped)

Beat eggs until light. Add sugar and beat well. Add the flour sifted with the baking powder. Add all-bran, nuts and dates. Spread mixture in a layer 1½ inch thick in a shallow greased pan. Bake in moderate oven (375°F.) for about 20 to 30 minutes. Remove from oven and cut into squares or bars white warm. Roll in powdered sugar or serve as a pudding with whipped cream. Pan size about 10"x15"

Date Hermits

3/4 cup of butter or shortening
2/3 cup brown sugar   1/2 teasp. vanilla
1 egg   2 cups flour
2 teasp. baking powder 1/2 teasp. salt
1 teasp. cinnamon   1/4 teasp. cloves
1/4 teasp. mace   1/2 teasp. nutmeg
1/4 cup milk   1 cup sliced dates

Cream sugar and butter or shortening. Add egg and vanilla. Mix well. Sift dry ingredients and add alternately with milk. Add dates. Drop by teaspoon onto greased baking sheet. Bake 20 minutes at 350°F.

Brown Sugar Macaroons

1 egg white   1 cup brown sugar
2 scant cups chopped pecans 1 teasp. vanilla

Beat egg white stiff. Beat in sugar. Add vanilla and pecans. Drop by teaspoon on well greased baking sheet. Bake in slow oven until brown. Coconut may be used in place of pecans.

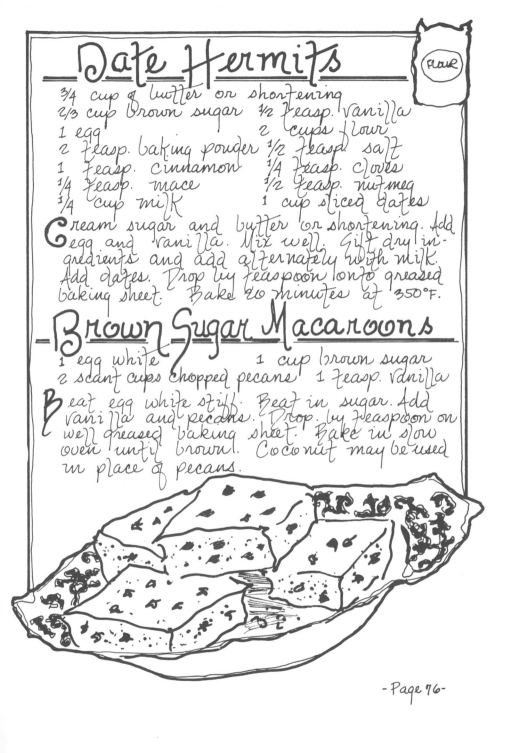

Old Fashioned Ginger Snaps

1 qt. best New Orleans molasses   3/4 lb. brown sugar
3/4 lb. lard & butter (1/2 & 1/2)   2 heaped teasp. soda
1 oz. ginger   1 oz cinnamon
1 oz. cloves   1/2 cup boiling water
        flour enough to make rather stiff dough.

Mix molasses, lard, and butter after having first warmed them to lukewarm temperature in separate vessels. Then add sugar gradually, beating the mixture all the time. Put soda into the 1/2 cup boiling water. Stir soda into water well, then stir this into mixture. Mix spices with some of the flour and stir in. Then add enough flour very gradually to make a dough about the consistency of bread dough. Set this dough in a cool place at least 24 hours to season before beginning to bake your cakes. Be sure to roll the dough very thin, and you will have ginger snaps that really snap! You do not have to bake all the dough at one time.

Corn Flake Macaroons

2 egg whites   1/2 cup brown sugar
1/2 teasp. Vanilla   2 cups corn flakes
1/2 cup chopped nuts   1 cup shredded coconut

Beat egg whites until stiff but not dry. Fold in sugar. Add flavoring, corn flakes, nut-meats, and coconut. Mix carefully. Drop by spoonfuls onto well greased baking sheet. Bake in moderate oven (350°F) for 15 to 20 minutes. Remove immediately from pan. Makes 2 dozen.

Apple Pie

1 1/2 cups of flour   1 teasp. salt
3 level Tbsp. shortening   4 Tbsp. ice water
6 apples   1 cup sugar
nutmeg & cinnamon   butter

Mix flour & salt. Put in shortening and then add ice water mix quickly as it will be very stiff. Roll thin crust and put in bottom of pie plate, 8 inches in size. You should have enough left for top crust.

Slice 6 apples, not too green not too ripe, into thin slices. Remove core and peeling. Arrange apple slices on un-cooked crust. Pile high as they will cook up. Then sprinkle sugar over them, dust flour from sifter, not much and add spices (nutmeg & cinnamon), dot with butter and add about 2 Table-spoons water. Put on top crust and crimp together. Cut cross in center to allow steam to escape. Cook in slow oven until apples feel tender when stuck. It will take an hour or longer depending on apples. (350°F)

French Apple Pie

8 medium size apples   1 9" pie shell unbaked
¼ cup flour   1 cup sugar
⅓ cup butter   ¼ teasp. nutmeg
½ teasp. allspice   ¼ teasp. cinnamon

Slice half the apples into the pie shell. Crumble flour, sugar, spices, and butter together. Sprinkle half of crumbs over apples---top with remaining sliced apples and cover with remaining crumbs. Place a cover (pot lid etc.) over pie and bake 30 minutes at 350°F. Remove cover and bake 30 minutes longer. Serve hot or cold. Pie is runny when hot.

Huguenot Tortes

2 eggs   1½ cups sugar
1 cup sliced apples   1 cup chopped nuts
4 Tbsp. flour   2½ teasp. baking powder
        2 teasp. vanilla

Beat eggs until foamy - - - - add sugar - - - flour - - - - - vanilla - - - apples, and nuts.

Bake in buttered pan (8"x16"x 2" deep) for 30 minutes in moderate oven (350°F). Top with whipped cream.
Will rise and fall. Serves 8

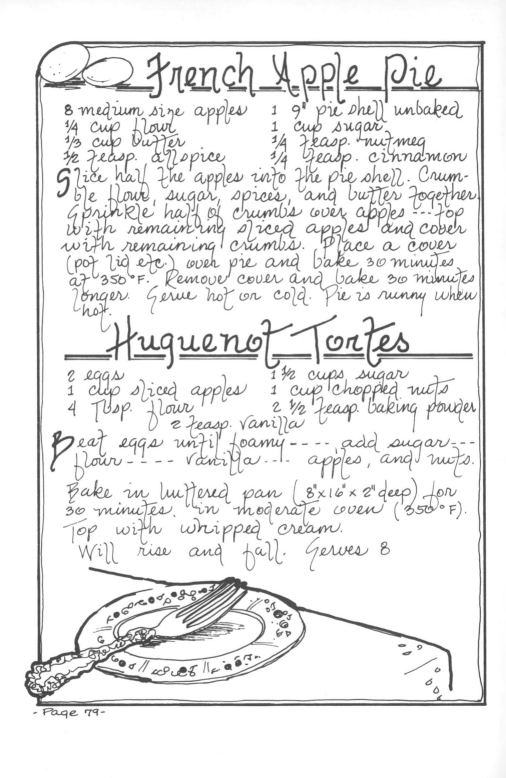

Pineapple Pie

½ cup sugar   6 Tbsp. flour
3 egg yolks   ⅛ Tbsp. salt
1 cup of drained grated pineapple.
3 Tbsp. butter   1¼ cups milk
          juice of ½ lemon

Mix sugar, salt, and flour together. Add pineapple, beaten egg yolks, butter and milk. Cook in double boiler until thick. Remove, add lemon juice and mix thoroughly. Cool. Pour in baked pie shell. Top with meringue. Brown.

Pecan Pie

4 eggs   1 cup sugar
1 cup white corn syrup 1 teasp. vanilla
2 Tbsp. butter   1 cup pecans (better if you use 2 cups of nuts) Good using mixed nuts too!!

Beat egg whites and yolks separately. Cream egg yolks, sugar, syrup, then add nuts & vanilla. Fold in egg whites stiffly beaten. Pour in unbaked pie shell. Cook in slow oven until done when tested with a silver knife.

Transparent Pie

½ cup butter   2 cups sugar
5 eggs   ½ teasp nutmeg (or
1 uncooked pie shell   juice of 1 lemon)

Cream the butter and sugar and add the eggs slightly beaten. Put in the chosen flavoring. Line individual pie pan (10in.) with pastry and pour in the mixture. Bake in a moderate oven (350°F.) for 20 to 30 minutes. This makes about 15 tarts or 1 pie.

Sweet Potatoe Custard

2 eggs   ¼ cup sugar
½ teasp. salt   ¼ teasp. nutmeg
1 teasp. grated orange rind 1¾ cups milk
1 Tbsp. melted butter   2½ cups of mashed
or shredded sweet potatoes. (cooked)

Beat the eggs, add sugar, salt, nutmeg, orange rind, and milk. Mix thoroughly, then add the sweet potatoes and butter to the custard mixture. Pour into unbaked pie shell and bake at 350° F. for about 50 minutes

Pumpkin Pie

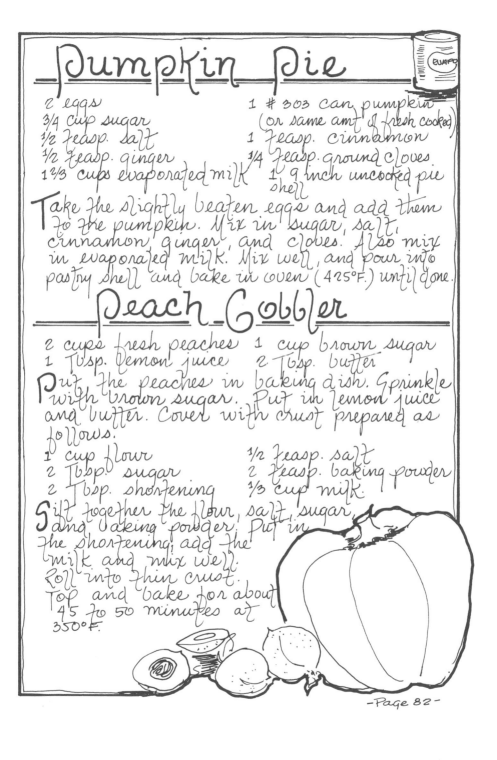

2 eggs
3/4 cup sugar
1/2 Teasp. salt
1/2 Teasp. ginger
1 2/3 cups evaporated milk

1 # 303 can pumpkin
(or same amt of fresh cooked)
1 Teasp. cinnamon
1/4 Teasp. ground cloves
1 9 inch uncooked pie shell

Take the slightly beaten eggs and add them to the pumpkin. Mix in sugar, salt, cinnamon, ginger, and cloves. Also mix in evaporated milk. Mix well, and pour into pastry shell and bake in oven (425°F.) until done.

Peach Cobbler

2 cups fresh peaches
1 Tbsp. lemon juice

1 cup brown sugar
2 Tbsp. butter

Put the peaches in baking dish. Sprinkle with brown sugar. Put in lemon juice and butter. Cover with crust prepared as follows.

1 cup flour
2 Tbsp. sugar
2 Tbsp. shortening

1/2 Teasp. salt
2 Teasp. baking powder
1/3 cup milk

Sift together the flour, salt, sugar, and baking powder. Put in the shortening, add the milk and mix well. Roll into thin crust. Top and bake for about 45 to 50 minutes at 350°F.

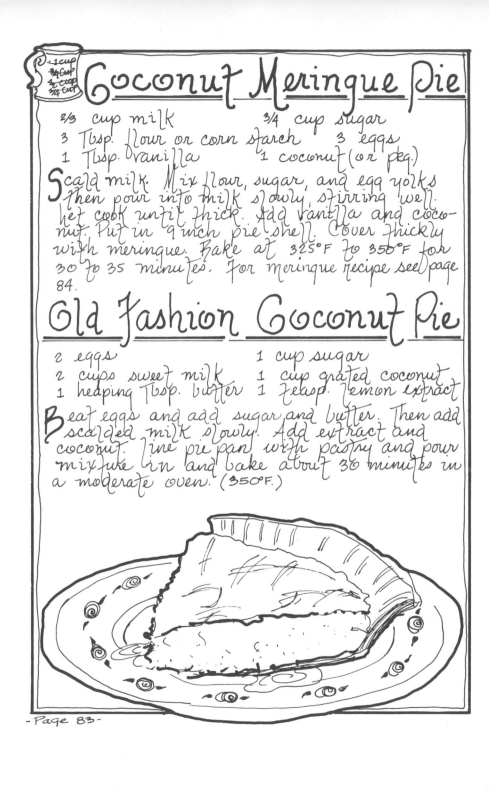

Coconut Meringue Pie

2/3 cup milk   3/4 cup sugar
3 Tbsp. flour or corn starch   3 eggs
1 Tbsp. vanilla   1 coconut (or pkg.)

Scald milk. Mix flour, sugar, and egg yolks
then pour into milk slowly, stirring well.
Let cook until thick. Add vanilla and coconut. Put in 9 inch pie shell. Cover thickly
with meringue. Bake at 325°F to 350°F for
30 to 35 minutes. For meringue recipe see page
84.

Old Fashion Coconut Pie

2 eggs   1 cup sugar
2 cups sweet milk   1 cup grated coconut
1 heaping Tbsp. butter 1 teasp. lemon extract

Beat eggs and add sugar and butter. Then add
scalded milk slowly. Add extract and
coconut. Line pie pan with pastry and pour
mixture in and bake about 30 minutes in
a moderate oven. (350°F.)

Coconut Cream Pie

½ cup sugar	5 Tbsp. flour
⅛ Teasp. salt	¼ cup cold milk
3 egg yolks	1 Teasp. vanilla
1 cup shredded coconut	1½ cups scalded milk

Blend sugar, flour, and salt with the cold milk. Add scalded milk stirring constantly. Cook on low heat until thick. Add beaten egg yolks, then cook 2 minutes longer. Remove from stove and add vanilla and coconut. Cool and pour into a 9 inch pie shell which has been baked previously. Cover top with meringue.

Meringue.

3 egg whites	6 level Tbsp. sugar

Beat egg whites stiff. They should be glossy on top, and when you turn the bowl up-side-down, they should remain in place. Fold in sugar gradually. Bake at 350° for 13 minutes

Lemon Meringue Pie

1 Tbsp. butter	1 cup sugar
3 egg yolks	2 Tbsp. milk
6 Tbsp. lemon juice	1 Teasp. grated rind
3 Tbsp. cold water	1¼ cups water
	¼ cup corn starch

Combine sugar, 1¼ C. water, & butter. Heat until sugar dissolves. Add corn starch mixed in 3 Tablespoons cold water. Cook slowly about 8 minutes or until clear. Add lemon juice and rind. Cook slowly 2 minutes. Add egg yolks beaten with milk. Bring to boiling point. Cool. Pour into baked pastry shell 8 or 9 inches. Spread with meringue made with 3 egg whites, beaten with 6 Tbsp. sugar & 1 Teasp. lemon juice. Brown in moderate oven.

Old Fashion Lemon Pie

2 eggs	1 cup sugar
juice & rind of 1 lemon	2 Tbsp. melted butter.
a pinch of salt	unbaked pie shell

Combine eggs, sugar, lemon juice and rind, melted butter, and salt. Mix well. Bake in an unbaked pie shell for about 1 hour starting at 275°F. and increasing to 300°F. Good.

Celestial Pie (lemon)

4 egg whites   1/4 teasp. salt
1/2 teasp. cream of tartar   1 cup sugar

Beat egg whites until foamy. Add salt and cream of tartar, and beat until stiff. Gradually add sugar until stiff enough to stand in peaks. It will be very stiff and glossy. Spread in 9 inch pie pan. Crust should be very thick in pan. Bake in a slow oven 275°F for 1 hour. Cool. Spread with lemon filling. The lemon filling can be substituted with cherry, peach, etc. This can be made into tart shells by spreading thick spoonfuls on waxed paper. Hollow a small place in the center for filling.

Filling:

1/2 cup flour   1 1/4 cups sugar
dash of salt   1 1/2 cups water
4 egg yolks (slightly beaten)   3/4 cup lemon juice
       1 Tbsp. grated lemon rind

Combine flour, sugar, and salt in the top of a double boiler. Add water and cook until clear like starch. Add egg yolks, slightly beaten. Cook until very thick. Remove from fire & add lemon juice & rind carefully. If too thin, cook longer. It thickens some as it cools. Cool. Pour into meringue.

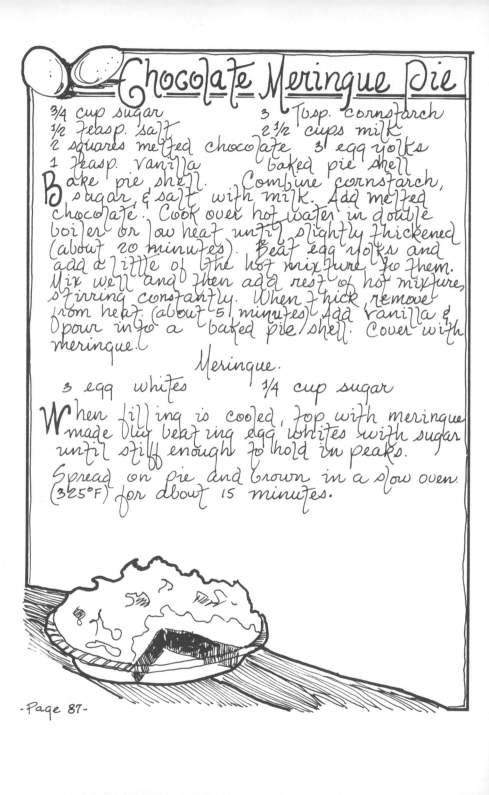

Chocolate Meringue Pie

3/4 cup sugar   3 Tbsp. cornstarch
1/2 Teasp. salt   2 1/2 cups milk
2 squares melted chocolate   3 egg yolks
1 Teasp. vanilla   baked pie shell

Bake pie shell. Combine cornstarch, sugar, & salt with milk. Add melted chocolate. Cook over hot water in double boiler or low heat until slightly thickened (about 20 minutes). Beat egg yolks and add a little of the hot mixture to them. Mix well and then add rest of hot mixture, stirring constantly. When thick, remove from heat (about 5 minutes) Add vanilla & pour into a baked pie shell. Cover with meringue.

Meringue.

3 egg whites   1/4 cup sugar

When filling is cooled, top with meringue made by beating egg whites with sugar until stiff enough to hold in peaks. Spread on pie and brown in a slow oven (325°F) for about 15 minutes.

My Own Quick Recipe for Chocolate Pie & the Pastry

For pie:

1 cup sweet milk   2 egg yolks
1/3 cup sugar   1½ heaping Tbsp. cocoa
2 heaping Tbsp. flour   1 bare pinch salt.

Beat eggs, add sugar, cocoa, & flour stirring constantly. When smooth, stir in milk. Cook in double boiler until thick. Pour into cooked pie crust and top with whipped cream when cool. (OR, whip whites of 2 eggs and add 2 tablespoons sugar. Smooth over pie and brown in moderate oven. (350°F.)

For pastry:

1 cup flour   ice water
shortening size of egg   greased pie pan

One cup of any kind flour (if plain add pinch of salt), creamed with shortening. Cream with knife or hand. Soften with ice water. Then knead until stiff enough to roll. Place in greased pie pan & trim edges. Take fork & pepper the whole thing into holes to avoid having bubbles. Bake until nearly done if you use meringue, and bake full done if you use whipped cream.

-Page 88-

Rice Pudding

1 cup rice (boiled till tender)
2 cups milk   2 eggs, separated
1 cup sugar (or little more) - pinch of salt
        1/4 stick butter

Beat egg yolks light. Add salt & sugar. Mix in
the butter. Stir in the milk. Add cooked
rice. Stir and flavor with vanilla. Fold
in the egg whites, stiffly beaten. Put
into greased pan and bake in 450° F. oven
until light brown.

Pioneer Bread Pudding

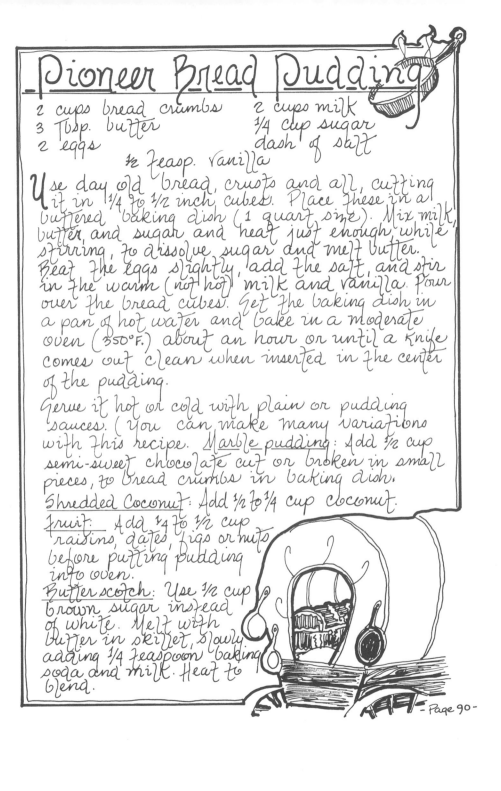

2 cups bread crumbs   2 cups milk
3 Tbsp. butter   1/4 cup sugar
2 eggs   dash of salt
½ teasp. vanilla

Use day old bread, crusts and all, cutting it in 1/4 to 1/2 inch cubes. Place these in a buttered baking dish (1 quart size). Mix milk, butter, and sugar and heat just enough, while stirring, to dissolve sugar and melt butter. Beat the eggs slightly, add the salt, and stir in the warm (not hot) milk and vanilla. Pour over the bread cubes. Set the baking dish in a pan of hot water and bake in a moderate oven (350°F.) about an hour or until a knife comes out clean when inserted in the center of the pudding.

Serve it hot or cold with plain or pudding sauces. (You can make many variations with this recipe. Marble pudding: Add ½ cup semi-sweet chocolate cut or broken in small pieces, to bread crumbs in baking dish.
Shredded Coconut: Add 1/2 to 1/4 cup coconut.
Fruit: Add 1/4 to 1/2 cup raisins, dates, figs or nuts before putting pudding into oven.
Butterscotch: Use 1/2 cup brown sugar instead of white. Melt with butter in skillet, slowly adding 1/4 teaspoon baking soda and milk. Heat to blend.

Date Pudding

1¼ cups chopped dates   1 cup sugar
1 cup nuts   1 teasp. soda
½ cup butter   1½ cups flour
1 cup boiling water   1 egg

Chop dates, sprinkle with soda, cover with boiling water and let stand until cool. Cream butter and sugar. Add egg, flour, cooled mixture, and nuts. Pour into greased baking dish and bake about 1 hour. (350°F.) Serve with whipped cream.

Pineapple Ice Box Pudding

2 egg yolks   ⅔ cup sugar
2 cups milk   1 cup pineapple juice
½ teasp. vanilla   1 cup crushed pineapple
Cornstarch in water (enough to thicken mixture)

Cream egg yolks and sugar together. Add milk and pineapple juice slowly. Add cornstarch mixed with water (approx. ½ cup.) until your custard is as thick as you wish. Be sure to cook custard slowly, stirring all the while.

Line a deep dish with vanilla wafers. Remove mixture from stove and add crushed pineapple and mix well. Now cover the vanilla wafers with custard until dish is about ⅔ is full. Allow your pudding mixture to cool and top with whipped cream. Place in ice box. (You may substitute any fruit you like)

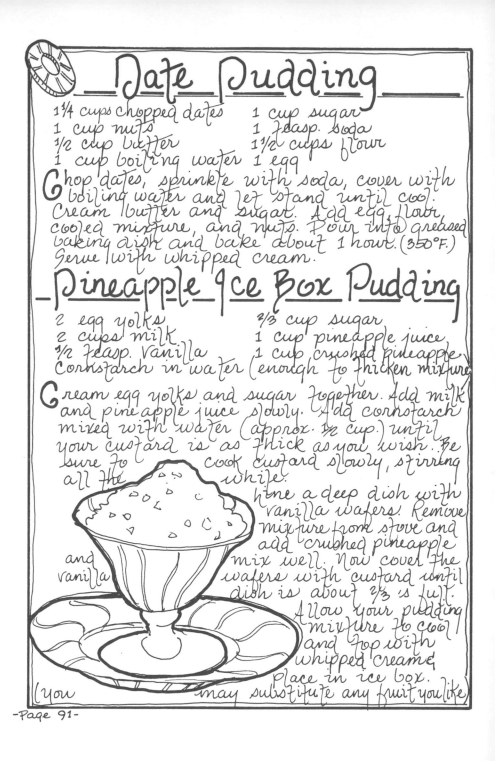

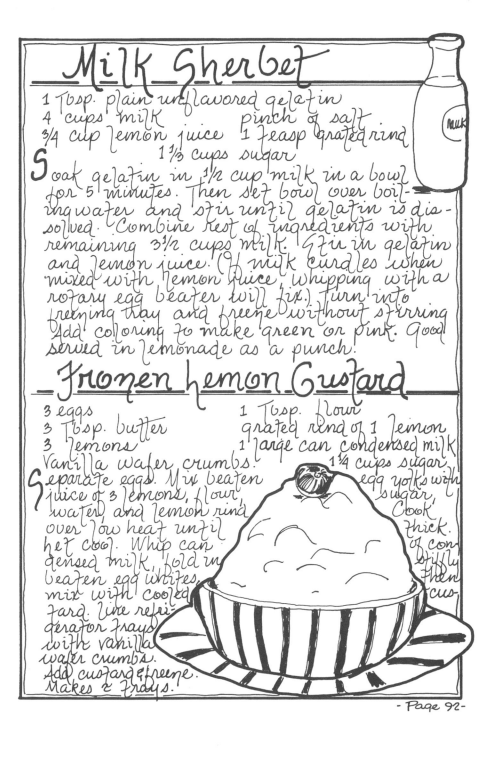

Milk Sherbet

1 Tbsp. plain unflavored gelatin
4 cups milk   pinch of salt
3/4 cup lemon juice 1 teasp grated rind
            1 1/3 cups sugar

Soak gelatin in 1/2 cup milk in a bowl for 5 minutes. Then set bowl over boiling water and stir until gelatin is dissolved. Combine rest of ingredients with remaining 3 1/2 cups milk. Stir in gelatin and lemon juice. (If milk curdles when mixed with lemon juice, whipping with a rotary egg beater will fix.) Turn into freezing tray and freeze without stirring. Add coloring to make green or pink. Good served in lemonade as a punch.

Frozen Lemon Custard

3 eggs   1 Tbsp. flour
3 Tbsp. butter   grated rind of 1 lemon
3 lemons   1 large can condensed milk
Vanilla wafer crumbs.   1 1/4 cups sugar

Separate eggs. Mix beaten egg yolks with juice of 3 lemons, flour, sugar, water, and lemon rind. Cook over low heat until thick. hot cool. Whip can of condensed milk, fold in stiffly beaten egg whites, then mix with cooled custard. Line refrigerator trays with vanilla wafer crumbs. Add custard & freeze. Makes 2 trays.

Grapefruit & Lime Sherbet

Cut grapefruit in halves. Remove center & seeds and pulp between sections. Leave grapefruit meat in halfs and refrigerate.

Lime sherbet

1 pkg. Lime gelatin	1 qt. sweet milk
juice of 2 lemons	1 cup boiling water

1½ cups sugar

Pour boiling water on gelatin. Add sugar & lemon juice. When cool add milk. Place in freezing tray. When half frozen beat well. This served on grapefruit halves makes a beautiful first course for a luncheon or dinner. Top with cherries.

Pineapple Sherbet

1 large can crushed pineapple · 2 cups water
juice of 4 lemons   3 pints of milk
Sugar to sweeten to taste (about 1 cup)

Mix sugar & water and bring to boil until sugar has dissolved. Set aside and let cool. Then add pineapple & lemon juice and mix well. Place in tray and freeze to a mush. Then add 3 pints milk, mix well. Freeze very hard. Serve.

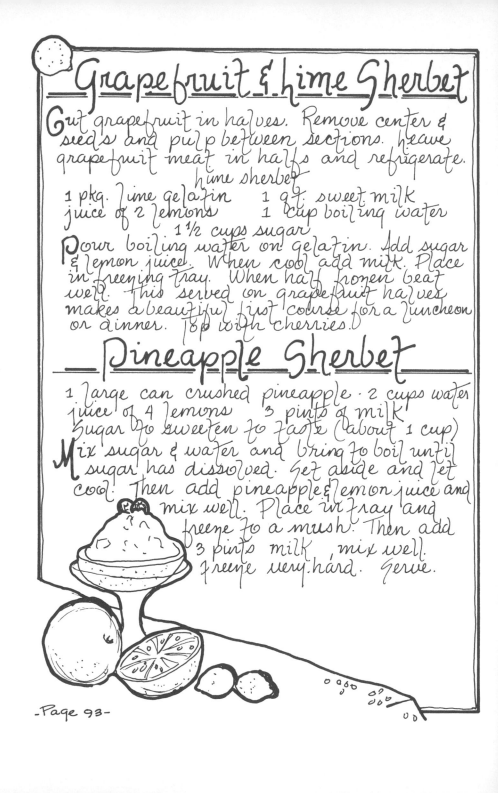

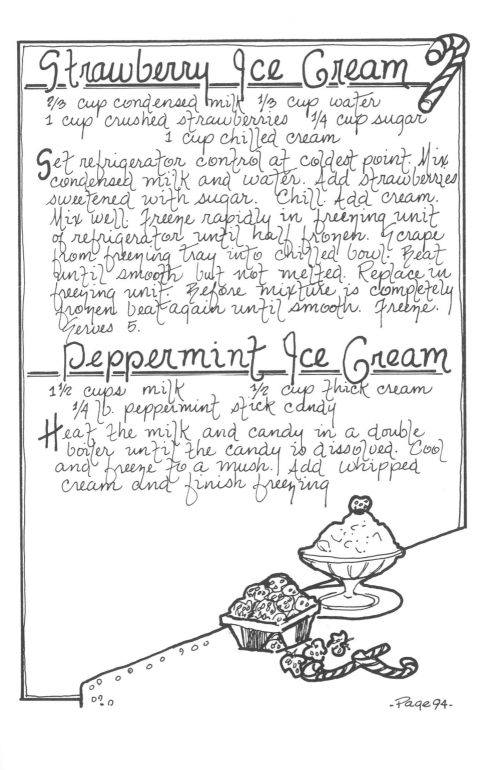

Strawberry Ice Cream

2/3 cup condensed milk 1/3 cup water
1 cup crushed strawberries 1/4 cup sugar
1 cup chilled cream

Set refrigerator control at coldest point. Mix condensed milk and water. Add strawberries sweetened with sugar. Chill. Add cream. Mix well. Freeze rapidly in freezing unit of refrigerator until half frozen. Scrape from freezing tray into chilled bowl. Beat until smooth but not melted. Replace in freezing unit. Before mixture is completely frozen beat again until smooth. Freeze. Serves 5.

Peppermint Ice Cream

1½ cups milk   ½ cup thick cream
1/4 lb. peppermint stick candy

Heat the milk and candy in a double boiler until the candy is dissolved. Cool and freeze to a mush. Add whipped cream and finish freezing

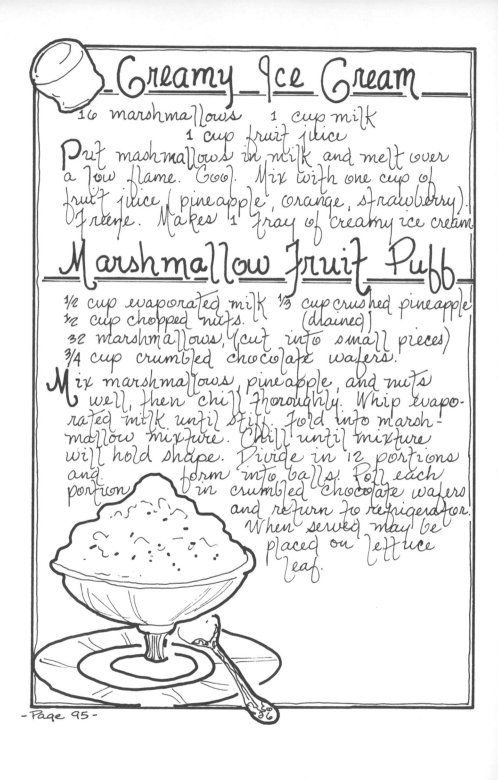

Creamy Ice Cream

16 marshmallows   1 cup milk
1 cup fruit juice

Put marshmallows in milk and melt over a low flame. Cool. Mix with one cup of fruit juice (pineapple, orange, strawberry). Freeze. Makes 1 tray of creamy ice cream.

Marshmallow Fruit Puff

½ cup evaporated milk   ⅓ cup crushed pineapple
½ cup chopped nuts.   (drained)
32 marshmallows, (cut into small pieces)
¾ cup crumbled chocolate wafers.

Mix marshmallows, pineapple, and nuts well, then chill thoroughly. Whip evaporated milk until stiff. Fold into marshmallow mixture. Chill until mixture will hold shape. Divide in 12 portions and form into balls. Roll each portion in crumbled chocolate wafers and return to refrigerator. When served may be placed on lettuce leaf.

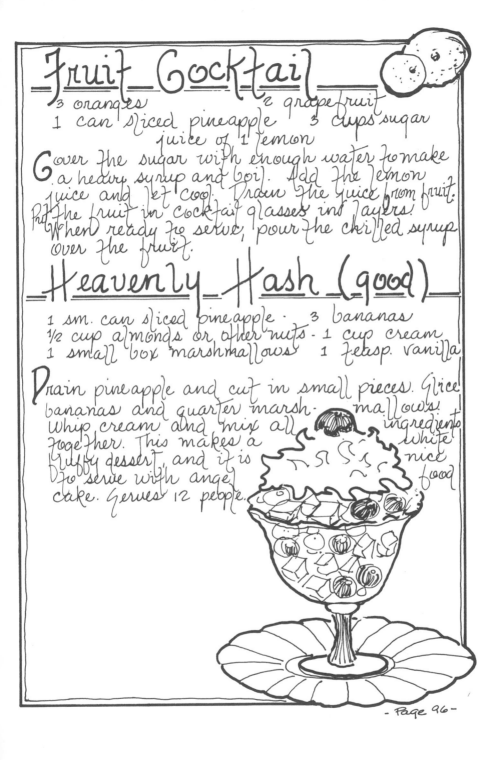

Fruit Cocktail

3 oranges   2 grapefruit
1 can sliced pineapple   3 cups sugar
              juice of 1 lemon

Cover the sugar with enough water to make a heavy syrup and boil. Add the lemon juice and let cool. Drain the juice from fruit. Put the fruit in cocktail glasses into layers. When ready to serve, pour the chilled syrup over the fruit.

Heavenly Hash (good)

1 sm. can sliced pineapple · 3 bananas
½ cup almonds or other nuts · 1 cup cream
1 small box marshmallows   1 teasp. vanilla

Drain pineapple and cut in small pieces. Slice bananas and quarter marshmallows. Whip cream and mix all ingredients together. This makes a fluffy dessert, and it is white nice to serve with angel food cake. Serves 12 people.

Strawberry Marlowe

1 cup crushed sweetened strawberries.
1 Tbsp. orange juice 3/4 lb. marshmallows
1/4 cup water   1 cup whipping cream
1/2 Teasp. vanilla   few grains salt.

Combine strawberries and orange juice. Combine marshmallows and water and cook over double boiler, stirring occasionally until melted. Fold into strawberry mixture. Cool. Whip cream slightly stiff and add vanilla and salt. Fold into strawberry mixture. Pour into freezing tray of refrigerator. Freeze firm. Serves 4.

Strawberry Pineapple Cup

3 cups hulled, washed strawberries
4 Tbsps. finely chopped mint leaves
1 1/2 cups of canned or fresh pineapple wedges
2/3 cup confectioners sugar

Place pineapple & strawberries in a large bowl in alternate layers. Sprinkle with sugar. Sprinkle mint over top and chill thoroughly. Serve in sherbet glasses. Serves 6

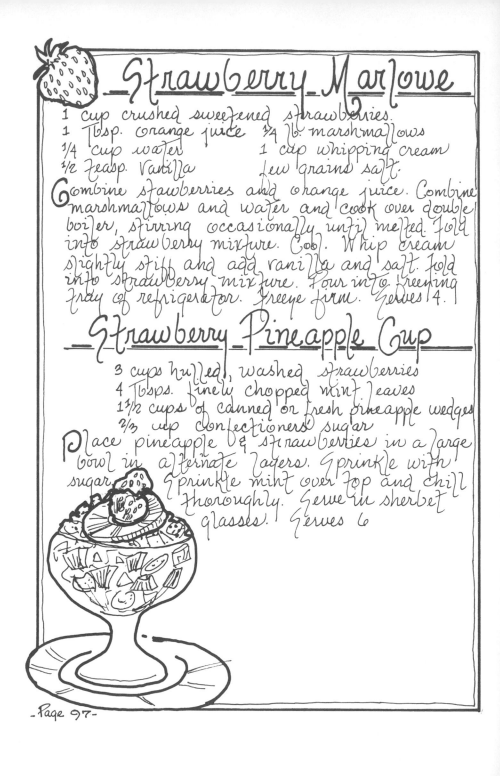

Pineapple Ice Box Dessert

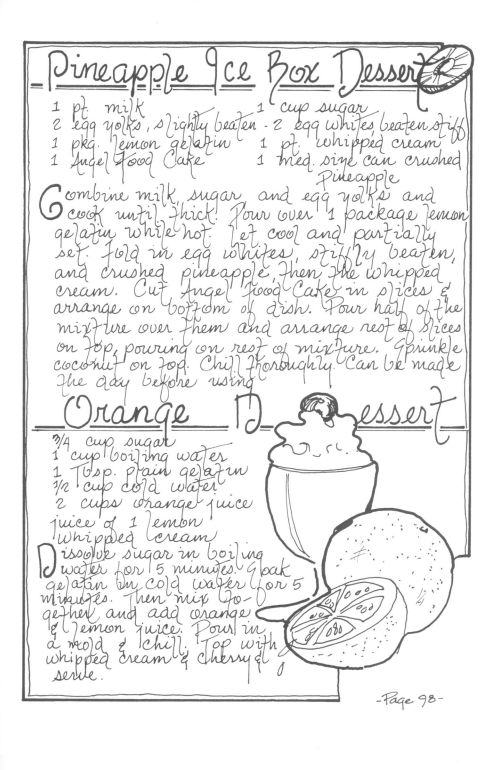

1 pt. milk   1 cup sugar
2 egg yolks, slightly beaten - 2 egg whites, beaten stiff
1 pkg. lemon gelatin   1 pt. whipped cream
1 Angel Food Cake   1 med. size can crushed
                                Pineapple

Combine milk, sugar and egg yolks and cook until thick. Pour over 1 package lemon gelatin while hot. Let cool and partially set. Fold in egg whites, stiffly beaten, and crushed pineapple, then the whipped cream. Cut Angel Food Cake in slices & arrange on bottom of dish. Pour half of the mixture over them and arrange rest of slices on top, pouring on rest of mixture. Sprinkle coconut on top. Chill thoroughly. Can be made the day before using.

Orange Dessert

3/4 cup sugar
1 cup boiling water
1 Tbsp. plain gelatin
1/2 cup cold water
2 cups orange juice
juice of 1 lemon
Whipped cream

Dissolve sugar in boiling water for 5 minutes. Soak gelatin in cold water for 5 minutes. Then mix together and add orange & lemon juice. Pour in a mold & chill. Top with whipped cream & cherry & serve.

Charlotte Russe I

1 cup milk	whites of 2 eggs
½ cup sugar	2 cups cream
2 Tbsp. gelatin	3 Tbsp. sherry wine
lady fingers or Pound cake	

Heat sugar & milk, saving out ¼ cup of milk in which to soak the gelatin. Dissolve the soaked gelatin mixture in hot milk. Beat the cream until stiff. Fold in the gelatin & milk mixture after cooling and flavor with wine. Fold in the beaten whites of 2 eggs. Line a mold with lady fingers or cake and when the Charlotte thickens put it in the mold and cover with more lady fingers. Chill thoroughly. May be prepared in individual servings

Charlotte Russe II

1 en. gelatin	4 egg whites
1 cup milk	1½ cups powdered sugar
1 pt. whipping cream	sponge cake
rose water or vanilla to taste	

Whip cream. Beat eggs to a stiff froth. Heat milk to boiling point & dissolve gelatin. Line a large mold with slices of sponge cake. Mix the gelatin, sugar, cream & flavoring together. Add lightly the frothed egg whites. Pour over the cake in the mold. Set away in ice box (do not freeze) until required for use. This is an easy & excellent mode of making this most delicate of desserts.

Charlotte Russe III

¼ cup powdered sugar · 1 pt. sweet cream
1 teasp. vanilla   sponge cake or lady fingers

Mix cream, sugar, & vanilla. Chill until very cold and whip to a stiff froth. Line dish with sponge cake or lady fingers. Fill with the whipped cream and serve cold.

Blanc Mange

½ box gelatin   1 qt. sweet milk
1 cup sugar   vanilla to taste
    whipped cream

Soak gelatin in as much cold water as will cover it until it dissolves. Boil milk and sugar just at boiling point 5 minutes, stirring constantly. Add gelatin mixture and boil 5 minutes more, still stirring. Flavor with vanilla, put into molds to cool and serve with whipped cream.

Chocolate Blanc Mange:

Add 4 oz. sweet chocolate grated to milk & sugar before heating. If wanted for tea make in the morning.

Lemon Fluff

2 eggs   1/2 cup sugar
1 Tbsp. sugar for egg whites   1 cup evaporated milk
vanilla wafers or Graham crackers crushed
juice of 1 lemon and the grated rind

Cook egg yolks, lemon juice, & sugar until thick. Let cool. Add to the whipped milk and egg whites. Place crushed wafers in a buttered dish. Add cooked mixture and top with crushed wafers. Chill & serve.

Ice Box Lime Dessert

1 pkg. lime gelatin   1 cup sugar
1 cup boiling water   1/2 cup cold water
juice of 2 lemons   1 can chilled evaporated
cracker crumbs   milk
                whipped cream

Dissolve gelatin in boiling water, add sugar & stir until dissolved. Add cold water. Let chill until looks like glue and whip. Add evaporated cream which has been whipped with lemon juice. Pour into plate lined with cracker crumbs. Serve with whipped cream.

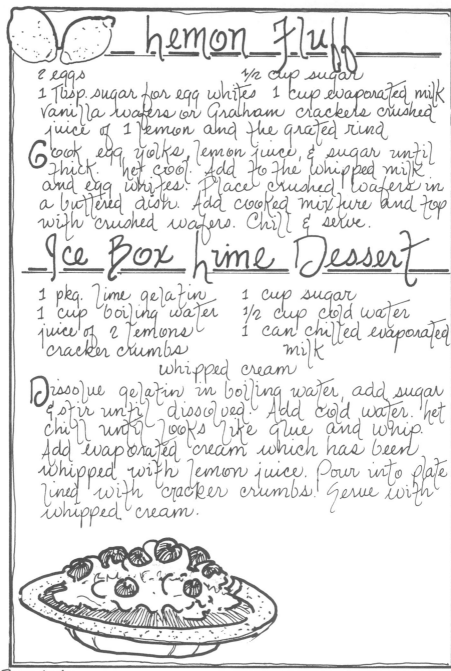

Syllabub

1 qt. cream   ½ pt. sweet wine
½ pt. Madeira   juice of two lemons
        spice and sugar to taste

Steep the peels of the lemon in the wine
to extract the flavor. Mix cream, sweet
wine, Madeira, and lemon juice and add
powdered spice and sugar to taste. Whisk
these ingredients together, removing the
froth with a spoon as it rises. Lay froth
on a fine sieve, whisking what drains
through, again. Put froth in glasses. Serves
12 people.

Floating Island

1 qt. milk   4 eggs
4 Tbsp. sugar   ¼ teasp. salt
½ cup currant jelly   2 teasp. vanilla or
                                          almond extract

Scald milk, but do not boil. Beat yolks of
eggs. Stir in sugar and salt. Add the hot
milk, mixing well. Cook slowly in sauce pan
(preferably over boiling water) until mixture
begins to thicken, stirring continually. When
cold, flavor and   put into
a rather shal-   low glass
dish. Make   meringue
of egg whites
whipped until
dry, into which
jelly has been beaten a teaspoonful
at a time. Heap meringue on
top of custard or drop   meringue with a
tablespoon to form "islands" and put small
pieces of jelly in center of each "island"
(Brown egg whites if you wish) Chill & serve.

Wine Marlowe

1 lb. mashmallows   1 cup hot wine
1 cup cream (rich)   crumb pastry

Dissolve mashmallows in hot wine and let cool. Whip cream and fold into marshmallow mixture. Put between crumb (vanilla or graham) pastry. Cut in squares to serve

Marshmallow Nut Delight

4 egg yolks   4 teasp. vinegar
4 Tbsp. sugar   ½ lb. marshmallows
1 small bottle cherries   8 slices pineapple
1 cup nuts   1 pt. whipped cream

Cook egg yolks, vinegar, and sugar until thick. Chop fruit and nuts and mix with sauce. Then mix with cream. Put in freezer and freeze.

Cream Puffs

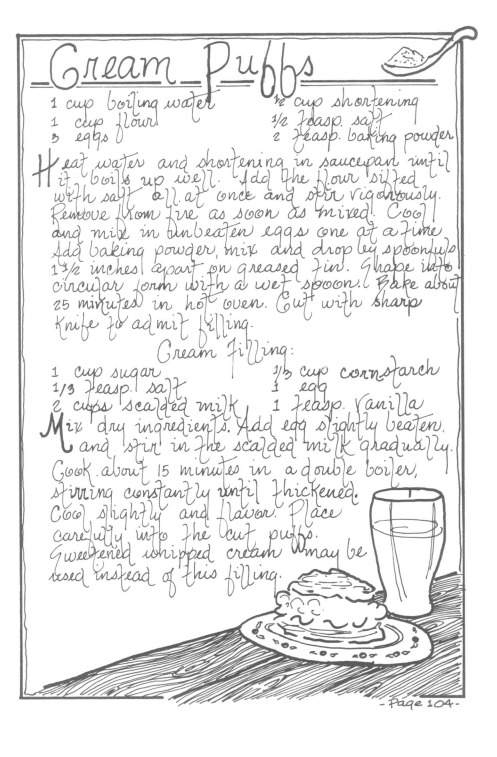

1 cup boiling water	½ cup shortening
1 cup flour	½ teasp. salt
3 eggs	2 teasp. baking powder

Heat water and shortening in saucepan until it boils up well. Add the flour sifted with salt all at once and stir vigorously. Remove from fire as soon as mixed. Cool and mix in unbeaten eggs one at a time. Add baking powder, mix and drop by spoonfuls 1½ inches apart on greased tin. Shape into circular form with a wet spoon. Bake about 25 minutes in hot oven. Cut with sharp knife to admit filling.

Cream Filling:

1 cup sugar	⅓ cup cornstarch
⅓ teasp. salt	1 egg
2 cups scalded milk	1 teasp. vanilla

Mix dry ingredients. Add egg slightly beaten and stir in the scalded milk gradually. Cook about 15 minutes in a double boiler, stirring constantly until thickened. Cool slightly and flavor. Place carefully into the cut puffs. Sweetened whipped cream may be used instead of this filling.

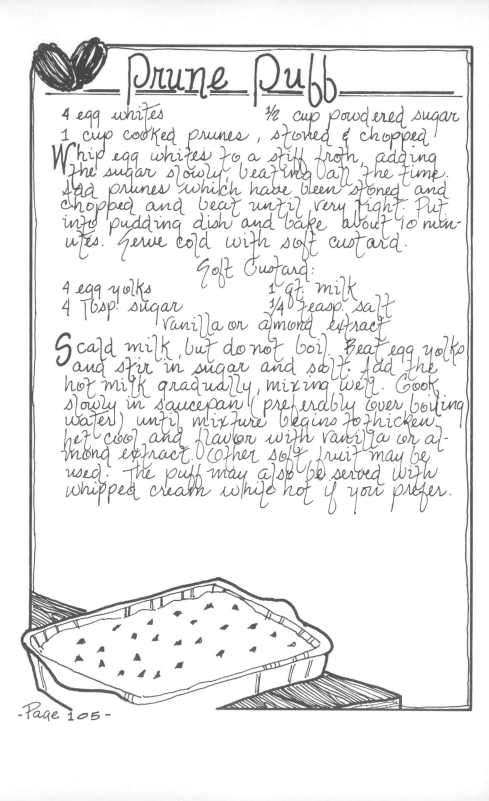

Prune Puff

4 egg whites   ½ cup powdered sugar
1 cup cooked prunes, stoned & chopped

Whip egg whites to a stiff froth, adding the sugar slowly, beating all the time. Add prunes which have been stoned and chopped and beat until very light. Put into pudding dish and bake about 10 minutes. Serve cold with soft custard.

Soft Custard:

4 egg yolks   1 qt. milk
4 Tbsp. sugar   ¾ teasp. salt
            Vanilla or almond extract

Scald milk, but do not boil. Beat egg yolks and stir in sugar and salt. Add the hot milk gradually, mixing well. Cook slowly in saucepan (preferably over boiling water) until mixture begins to thicken. Let cool and flavor with vanilla or almond extract. Other soft fruit may be used. The puff may also be served with whipped cream while hot if you prefer.

Baked Apple Dumplings

1 pkg of dried apples   Sugar
            biscuit dough

Cook one package of dried apples until done. Sweeten to taste. Take pieces of good biscuit dough the size of a walnut and roll out until thin. Put about 2 Tablespoons of apples in center and fold over, forming a large biscuit. Arrange in deep pan or plate, brown in oven. Have ready a butter sauce, and pour over apple dumplings when taken from oven.

Butter Sauce:

4 Tbsp. butter	3 Tbsp. sugar
1 teasp. vanilla	2 cups hot water

Put butter and sugar together in the 2 cups of hot boiling water, stirring until butter & sugar dissolve. Add vanilla, then pour over baked apple dumplings. Serve (Real Good)

White House Punch

1 bottle white wine	8 oz. good brandy
2 qts. ginger ale	juice of 6 lemons
8 Tbsp. sugar	1 cup water

Boil sugar in 1 cup of water for 10 minutes or until syrupy. When cool add lemon juice. Just before serving add wine, brandy and ginger ale. Serves 20

"Recipe was given to my mother by Joseph, a true butler at the White House."

The above note was written at the bottom of the original recipe.

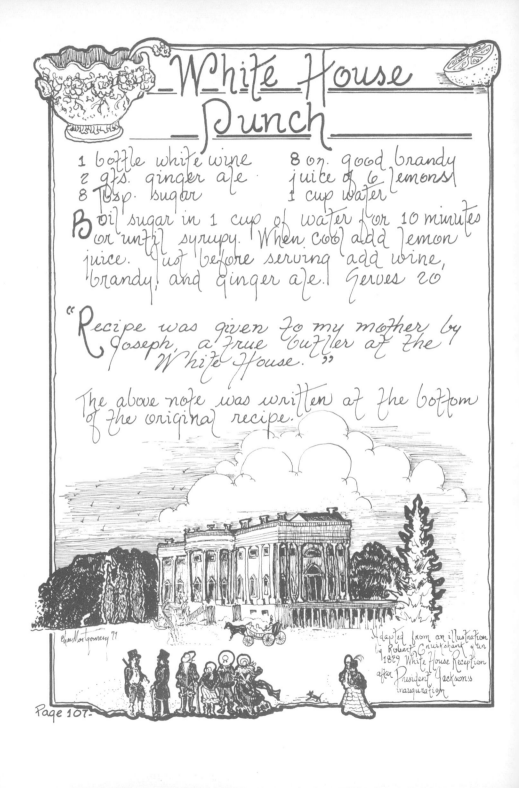

ChuMontgomery '71

Adapted from an illustration by Robert Cruikshank of an 1829 White House Reception after President Jackson's inauguration

Russian Tea

juice of 4 oranges   juice of 3 or 4 lemons
3/4 cup sugar   1 cup water
3 pts. hot tea   1 teasp. whole cloves
Dissolve sugar in water. Mix with
fruit juices and add to tea. Drop in cloves
and let simmer until served. (serves 10)

Russian Tea (serves 30)

1 gallon freshly made tea   1 cup lemon juice
1 cup orange juice   2 cups sugar
2 Tbsp. whole cloves

Prepare same as above.

Black & White Candy

½ pared raw medium potatoe
2 cups sifted confectioner's sugar
¾ lb. package of shredded coconut
2 sgs. (2 oz.) unsweetened chocolate

Boil potatoe until tender, drain. Dry potatoe slightly by shaking over heat. Mash. Then add sugar, coconut. Beat well with a spoon. Put into greased 8" by 8" by 2" pan. Cool. Spread with melted chocolate. Cool well, cut in squares. Wrap in waxed paper. Makes about 1 pound.

Kisses

1 cup sugar
1 cup of nut meats
4 egg whites
pinch of salt
flavoring
almond or vanilla extract

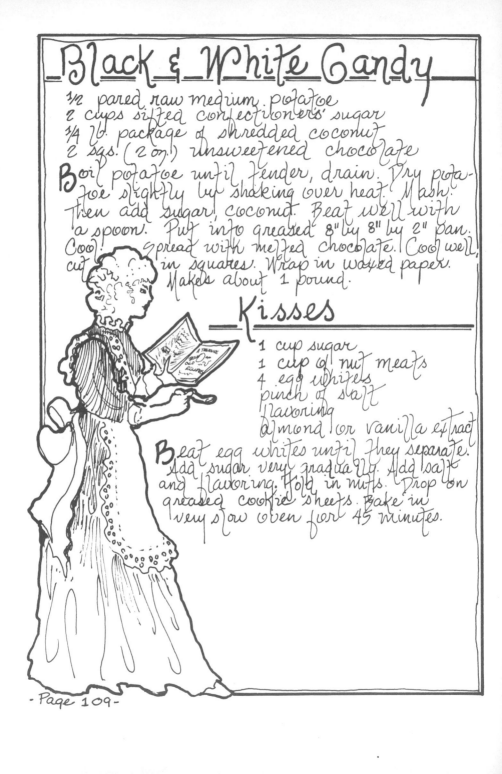

Beat egg whites until they separate. Add sugar very gradually. Add salt and flavoring. Hold in nuts. Drop on greased cookie sheets. Bake in very slow oven for 45 minutes.

Date Nut Roll Candy

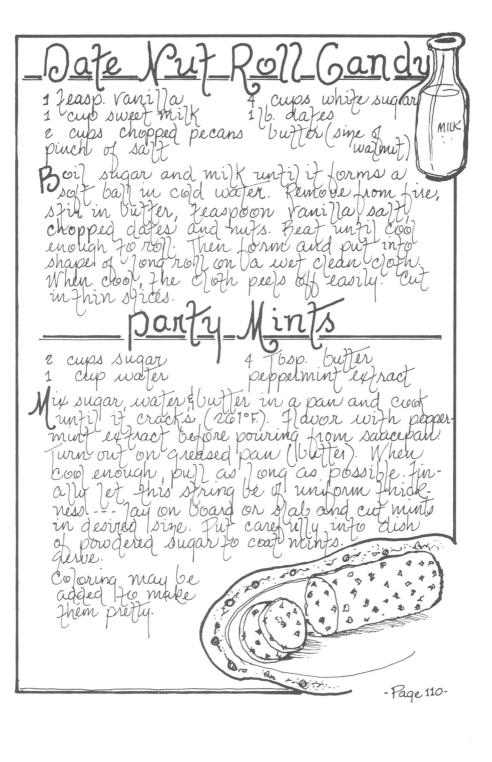

1 teasp. vanilla
1 cup sweet milk
2 cups chopped pecans
pinch of salt

4 cups white sugar
1 lb. dates
butter (size of walnut)

Boil sugar and milk until it forms a soft ball in cold water. Remove from fire, stir in butter, teaspoon vanilla, salt, chopped dates and nuts. Beat until cool enough to roll. Then form and put into shape of long roll on a wet clean cloth. When cool, the cloth peels off easily. Cut in thin slices.

Party Mints

2 cups sugar
1 cup water

4 Tbsp. butter
peppermint extract

Mix sugar, water & butter in a pan and cook until it cracks (261°F.). Flavor with peppermint extract before pouring from saucepan. Turn out on greased pan (butter). When cool enough, pull as long as possible. Finally let this string be of uniform thickness --- Lay on board or slab and cut mints in desired size. Put carefully into dish of powdered sugar to coat mints. Serve.

Coloring may be added to make them pretty.

Divinity Candy

3½ cups sugar   1 cup water
½ cup corn syrup   2 egg whites
½ lb. shelled pecans   Vanilla extract

Add sugar to water and put on stove. When it reaches boiling stage, add corn syrup. Have ready the well beaten egg whites, & when syrup threads as thin as a hair when dropped from a spoon, pour 5 tablespoons full over whites, beating constantly. Put remainder of syrup back on stove and allow it to cook until it forms a hard ball when dropped into cold water, then pour over whites. Beat well, flavor with vanilla and add pecans. Candy should be dropped on waxed paper from teaspoon to harden & each piece may be topped with a pecan half if desired.

Sea Foam Candy

2 cups brown sugar   1 cup cold water
1 teasp. vinegar   1 egg white

Cook sugar and water until it forms a soft ball in water. Then add vinegar and pour it on the well beaten egg whites. Beat candy until it will hold its shape like a bon-bon when dropped from a spoon.

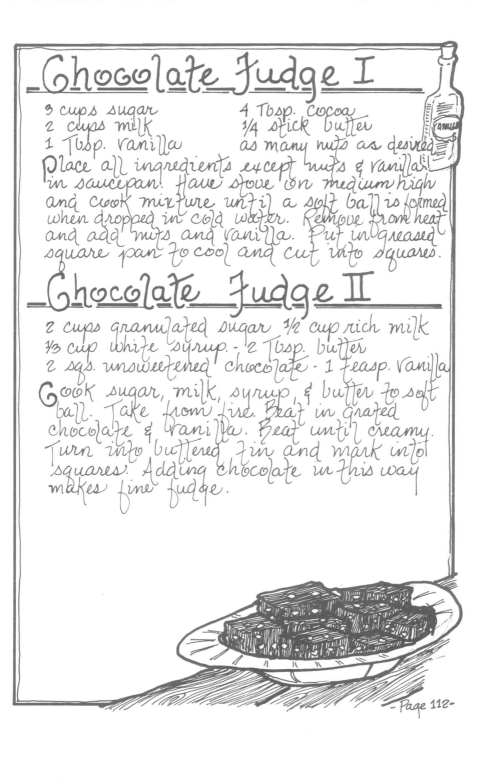

Chocolate Fudge I

3 cups sugar   4 Tbsp. cocoa
2 cups milk   1/4 stick butter
1 Tbsp. vanilla   as many nuts as desired

Place all ingredients except nuts & vanilla
in saucepan. Have stove on medium high
and cook mixture until a soft ball is formed
when dropped in cold water. Remove from heat
and add nuts and vanilla. Put in greased
square pan to cool and cut into squares.

Chocolate Fudge II

2 cups granulated sugar 1/2 cup rich milk
1/3 cup white syrup. - 2 Tbsp. butter
2 sqs. unsweetened chocolate - 1 teasp. vanilla

Cook sugar, milk, syrup, & butter to soft
ball. Take from fire. Beat in grated
chocolate & vanilla. Beat until creamy.
Turn into buttered tin and mark into
squares. Adding chocolate in this way
makes fine fudge.

Baked Asparagus

2 Tbsp. shortening (butter) - 2 Tbsp. sugar
1 cup milk - 2 cups cooked or canned asparagus
½ teasp. salt   add dusting of white pepper
1½ cup grated tart cheese - hard-boiled eggs
½ cup browned bread crumbs or crushed saltines
pimentos - 2 Tbsp. flour - paprika to taste

Make a cream sauce of shortening, flour, salt, pepper, and milk. Add cheese and let melt in sauce. Blend the asparagus with the sauce. Pour into well oiled baking dish. Top with coating of crumbs or crackers. Place in hot oven until bubbling hot. Garnish with hard-boiled egg and pimento slices. Dust with paprika. Serve hot.

Asparagus Au Gratin

Creamed asparagus   grated cheese
butter   Uneeda Crackers or
                            crumbs.

Arrange creamed asparagus in buttered baking dish. Sprinkle with buttered Uneeda crackers or crumbs and bake until crumbs are brown. Grated cheese may be mixed with crumbs.

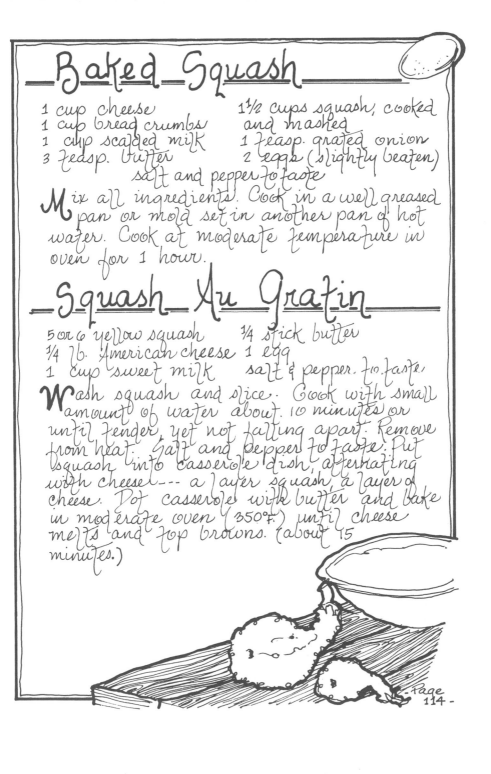

Baked Squash

1 cup cheese
1 cup bread crumbs
1 cup scalded milk
3 teasp. butter

1½ cups squash, cooked and mashed
1 teasp. grated onion
2 eggs (slightly beaten)

salt and pepper to taste

Mix all ingredients. Cook in a well greased pan or mold set in another pan of hot water. Cook at moderate temperature in oven for 1 hour.

Squash Au Gratin

5 or 6 yellow squash
¼ lb. American cheese
1 cup sweet milk

¼ stick butter
1 egg
salt & pepper. to taste.

Wash squash and slice. Cook with small amount of water about 10 minutes or until tender, yet not falling apart. Remove from heat. Salt and pepper to taste. Put squash into casserole dish, alternating with cheese--- a layer squash, a layer of cheese. Dot casserole with butter and bake in moderate oven (350°F.) until cheese melts and top browns. (about 15 minutes.)

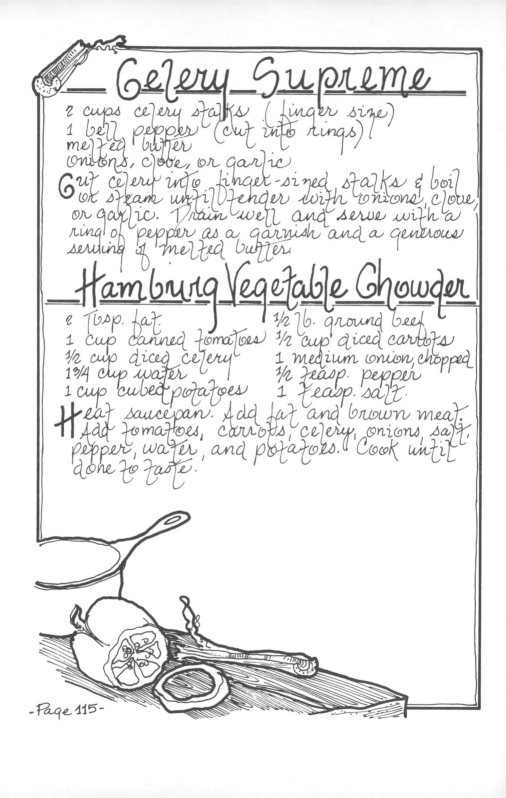

Celery Supreme

2 cups celery stalks (finger size)
1 bell pepper (cut into rings)
melted butter
onions, clove, or garlic

Cut celery into finger-sized stalks & boil
or steam until tender with onions, clove,
or garlic. Drain well and serve with a
ring of pepper as a garnish and a generous
serving of melted butter.

Hamburg Vegetable Chowder

2 Tbsp. fat   ½ lb. ground beef
1 cup canned tomatoes   ½ cup diced carrots
½ cup diced celery   1 medium onion, chopped
1¾ cup water   ½ teasp. pepper
1 cup cubed potatoes   1 teasp. salt.

Heat saucepan. Add fat and brown meat.
Add tomatoes, carrots, celery, onions, salt,
pepper, water, and potatoes. Cook until
done to taste.

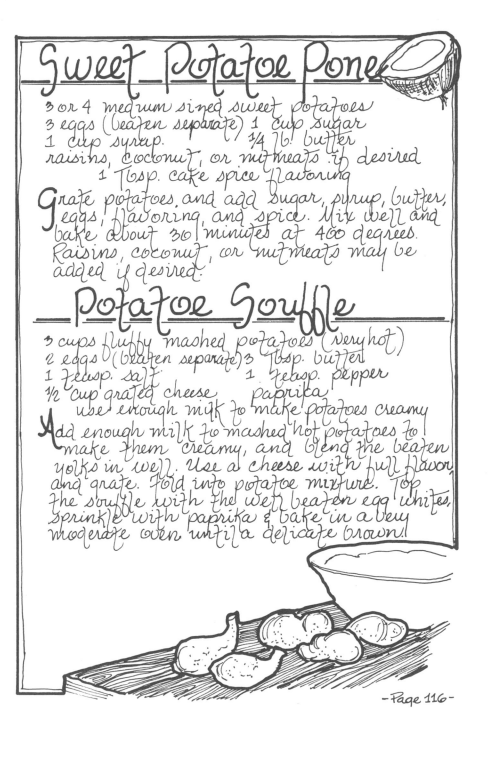

Sweet Potatoe Pone

3 or 4 medium sized sweet potatoes
3 eggs (beaten separate) 1 cup sugar
1 cup syrup.   1/4 lb. butter
raisins, coconut, or nutmeats if desired
        1 Tbsp. cake spice flavoring

Grate potatoes and add sugar, syrup, butter,
eggs, flavoring, and spice. Mix well and
bake about 30 minutes at 400 degrees.
Raisins, coconut, or nutmeats may be
added if desired.

Potatoe Souffle

3 cups fluffy mashed potatoes (very hot)
2 eggs (beaten separate) 3 Tbsp. butter
1 teasp. salt   1 teasp. pepper
1/2 cup grated cheese   paprika
    use enough milk to make potatoes creamy

Add enough milk to mashed hot potatoes to
make them creamy, and blend the beaten
yolks in well. Use a cheese with full flavor,
and grate. Fold into potatoe mixture. Top
the souffle with the well beaten egg whites,
sprinkle with paprika & bake in a very
moderate oven until a delicate brown.

Macaroni Pie

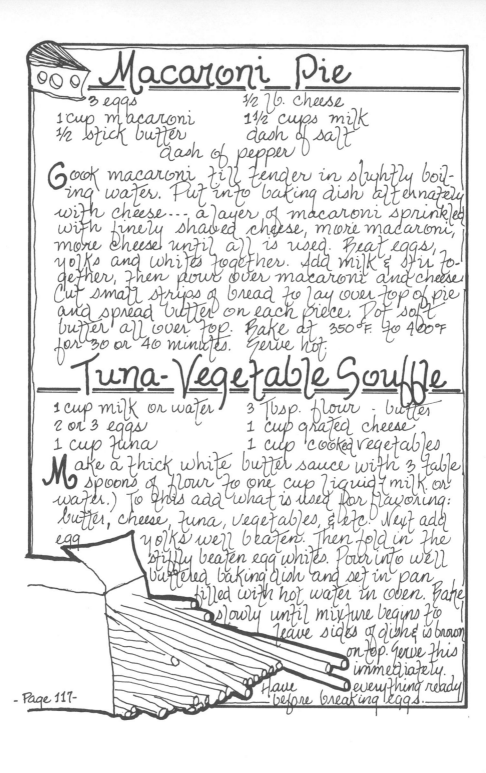

3 eggs   ½ lb. cheese
1 cup macaroni   1½ cups milk
½ stick butter   dash of salt
        dash of pepper

Cook macaroni till tender in slightly boiling water. Put into baking dish alternately with cheese--- a layer of macaroni sprinkled with finely shaved cheese, more macaroni, more cheese until all is used. Beat eggs, yolks and whites together. Add milk & stir together, then pour over macaroni and cheese. Cut small strips of bread to lay over top of pie and spread butter on each piece. Pot soft butter all over top. Bake at 350°F. to 400°F for 30 or 40 minutes. Serve hot.

Tuna-Vegetable Souffle

1 cup milk or water   3 Tbsp. flour - butter
2 or 3 eggs   1 cup grated cheese
1 cup tuna   1 cup cooked vegetables

Make a thick white butter sauce with 3 tablespoons of flour to one cup liquid (milk or water.) To this add what is used for flavoring: butter, cheese, tuna, vegetables, & etc. Next add egg yolks well beaten. Then fold in the stiffly beaten egg whites. Pour into well buttered baking dish and set in pan filled with hot water in oven. Bake slowly until mixture begins to leave sides of dish & is brown on top. Serve this immediately. Have everything ready before breaking eggs.

Eggplant Casserole

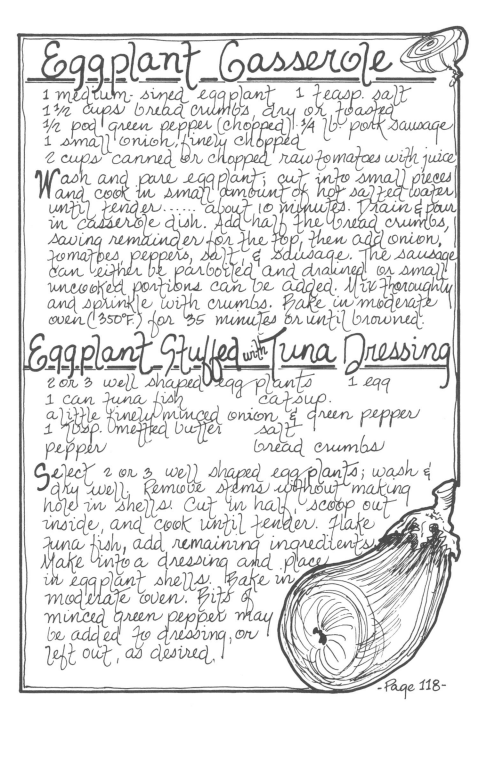

1 medium-sized eggplant   1 teasp. salt
1½ cups bread crumbs, dry or toasted
½ pod green pepper (chopped). ¾ lb. pork sausage
1 small onion, finely chopped
2 cups canned or chopped raw tomatoes with juice

Wash and pare eggplant; cut into small pieces and cook in small amount of hot salted water until tender...... about 10 minutes. Drain & pour in casserole dish. Add half the bread crumbs, saving remainder for the top, then add onion, tomatoes, peppers, salt & sausage. The sausage can either be parboiled and drained or small uncooked portions can be added. Mix thoroughly and sprinkle with crumbs. Bake in moderate oven (350°F.) for 35 minutes or until browned.

Eggplant Stuffed with Tuna Dressing

2 or 3 well shaped egg plants   1 egg
1 can tuna fish   catsup.
a little finely minced onion & green pepper
1 tbsp. melted butter   salt
pepper   bread crumbs

Select 2 or 3 well shaped egg plants; wash & dry well. Remove stems without making hole in shells. Cut in half, scoop out inside, and cook until tender. Flake tuna fish, add remaining ingredients. Make into a dressing and place in eggplant shells. Bake in moderate oven. Bits of minced green pepper may be added to dressing, or left out, as desired.

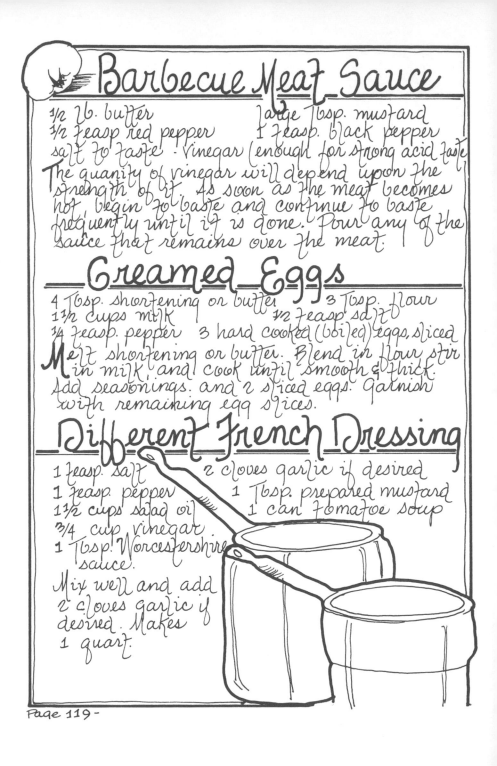

Barbecue Meat Sauce

½ lb. butter   large Tbsp. mustard
½ teasp red pepper   1 teasp. black pepper
salt to taste . vinegar (enough for strong acid taste
The quanity of vinegar will depend upon the
strength of it. As soon as the meat becomes
hot, begin to baste and continue to baste
frequently until it is done. Pour any of the
sauce that remains over the meat.

Creamed Eggs

4 Tbsp. shortening or butter   3 Tbsp. flour
1½ cups milk   ½ teasp salt
¼ teasp. pepper   3 hard cooked (boiled) eggs, sliced
Melt shortening or butter. Blend in flour stir
in milk, and cook until smooth & thick.
Add seasonings. and 2 sliced eggs. Garnish
with remaining egg slices.

Different French Dressing

1 teasp. salt   2 cloves garlic if desired
1 teasp. pepper   1 Tbsp. prepared mustard
1½ cups salad oil   1 can tomatoe soup
¾ cup vinegar
1 Tbsp. Worcestershire
     sauce.

Mix well and add
2 cloves garlic if
desired. Makes
1 quart.

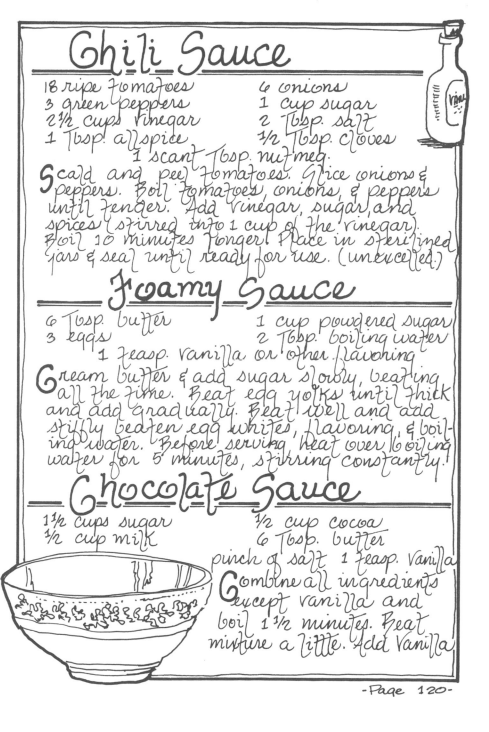

Chili Sauce

18 ripe Tomatoes	6 onions
3 green peppers	1 cup sugar
2½ cups vinegar	2 Tbsp. salt
1 Tbsp. allspice	½ Tbsp. cloves

1 scant Tbsp. nutmeg.

Scald and peel Tomatoes. Slice onions & peppers. Boil Tomatoes, onions, & peppers until tender. Add vinegar, sugar, and spices (stirred into 1 cup of the vinegar). Boil 10 minutes longer. Place in sterilized jars & seal until ready for use. (unexcelled.)

Foamy Sauce

6 Tbsp. butter	1 cup powdered sugar
3 eggs	2 Tbsp. boiling water

1 teasp. vanilla or other flavoring

Cream butter & add sugar slowly, beating all the time. Beat egg yolks until thick and add gradually. Beat well and add stiffly beaten egg whites, flavoring, & boiling water. Before serving, heat over boiling water for 5 minutes, stirring constantly.

Chocolate Sauce

1½ cups sugar	½ cup cocoa
½ cup milk	6 Tbsp. butter

pinch of salt   1 teasp. vanilla

Combine all ingredients except vanilla and boil 1½ minutes. Beat mixture a little. Add vanilla

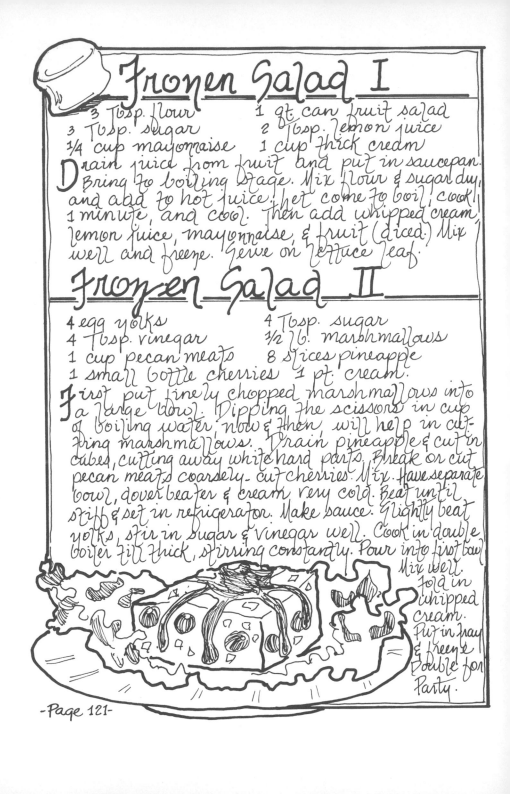

Frozen Salad I

3 Tbsp. flour	1 qt. can fruit salad
3 Tbsp. sugar	2 Tbsp. lemon juice
1/4 cup mayonnaise	1 cup thick cream

Drain juice from fruit and put in saucepan. Bring to boiling stage. Mix flour & sugar dry, and add to hot juice. Let come to boil, cook 1 minute, and cool. Then add whipped cream, lemon juice, mayonnaise, & fruit (diced.) Mix well and freeze. Serve on lettuce leaf.

Frozen Salad II

4 egg yolks	4 Tbsp. sugar
4 Tbsp. vinegar	1/2 lb. marshmallows
1 cup pecan meats	8 slices pineapple
1 small bottle cherries	1 pt. cream

First put finely chopped marshmallows into a large bowl. Dipping the scissors in cup of boiling water, now & then, will help in cutting marshmallows. Drain pineapple & cut in cubes, cutting away white hard parts. Break or cut pecan meats coarsely. Cut cherries. Mix. Have separate bowl, dover beater & cream very cold. Beat until stiff & set in refrigerator. Make sauce. Slightly beat yolks, stir in sugar & vinegar well. Cook in double boiler till thick, stirring constantly. Pour into first bowl. Mix well. Fold in whipped cream. Put in tray & freeze. Double for Party.

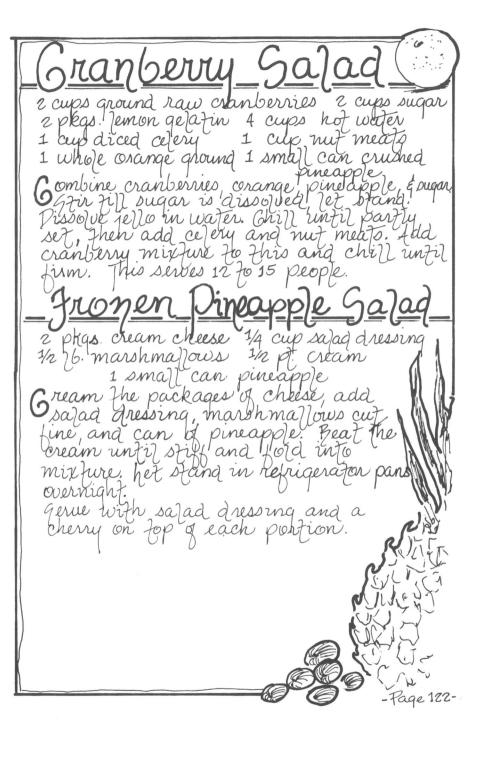

Cranberry Salad

2 cups ground raw cranberries   2 cups sugar
2 pkgs. lemon gelatin   4 cups hot water
1 cup diced celery   1 cup nut meats
1 whole orange ground   1 small can crushed
                                pineapple

Combine cranberries, orange, pineapple, & sugar.
Stir till sugar is dissolved, let stand.
Dissolve jello in water. Chill until partly
set, then add celery and nut meats. Add
cranberry mixture to this and chill until
firm. This serves 12 to 15 people.

Frozen Pineapple Salad

2 pkgs. cream cheese   1/4 cup salad dressing
1/2 lb. marshmallows   1/2 pt. cream
            1 small can pineapple

Cream the packages of cheese, add
salad dressing, marshmallows cut
fine, and can of pineapple. Beat the
cream until stiff and fold into
mixture. Let stand in refrigerator pans
overnight.
Serve with salad dressing and a
cherry on top of each portion.

Cherry Salad

1 can pie cherries	juice from cherries
1 cup sugar	1 pkg. lemon gelatin
1 teasp. plain gelatin	1 small can crushed
juice & rind of 1 orange	pineapple
juice & rind of 1 lemon	

Heat cherry juice & add sugar. Prepare lemon gelatin as directed on package, and add 1 teaspoonful of plain gelatin. Add to juice mixture along with fruit and grated rinds. Mix well and chill until firm.

24·Hour Fruit Salad

2 egg yolks	¼ cup sugar
¼ cup cream	juice of 2 lemons
⅛ teasp. salt	1 cup chopped pecans
½ lb. marshmallows (cut up)	1 cup heavy cream (whipped)
6 slices of canned pineapple (diced)	
2 cups Queen Anne Cherries (stoned)	
½ lb. grapes (peeled & seeded) (optional)	

Put into double boiler egg yolks, sugar, cream, juice of two lemons, salt and cook until thick, stirring constantly. Chill and add pineapple, cherries, grapes, pecans, marshmallows and whipped cream. Chill the salad for 24 hours to enhance flavor, then serve it on lettuce with mayonnaise for salad or as a dessert with whipped cream. Makes 12 to 14 servings.

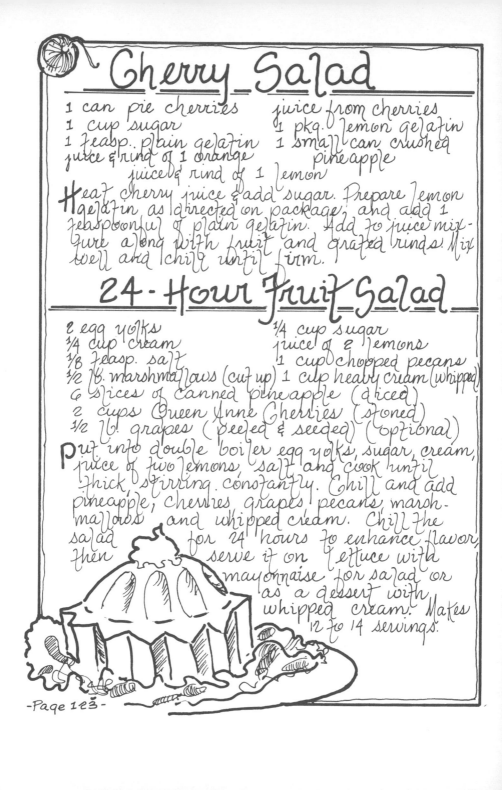

Fruit Salad

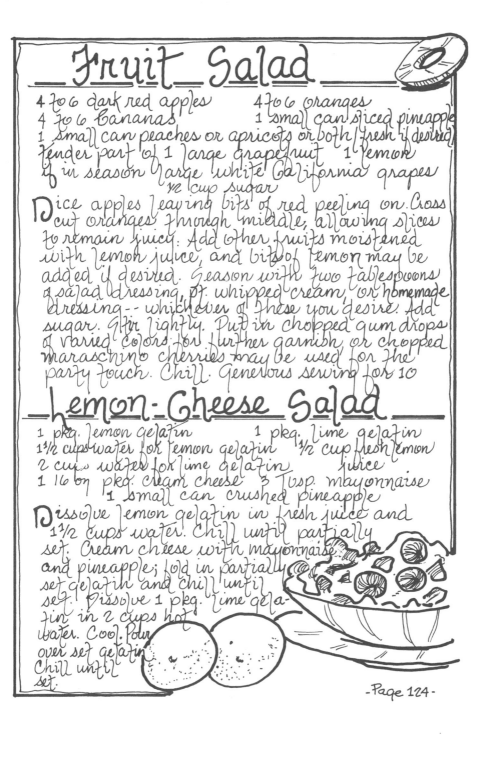

4 to 6 dark red apples　　4 to 6 oranges
4 to 6 bananas　　1 small can sliced pineapple
1 small can peaches or apricots or both/fresh if desired
Tender part of 1 large grapefruit　1 lemon
If in season large white California grapes
½ cup sugar

Dice apples leaving bits of red peeling on. Cross cut oranges through middle, allowing slices to remain juicy. Add other fruits moistened with lemon juice, and bits of lemon may be added if desired. Season with two tablespoons of salad dressing, pt. whipped cream, or homemade dressing-- whichever of these you desire. Add sugar. Stir lightly. Put in chopped gum drops of varied colors for further garnish or chopped maraschino cherries may be used for the party touch. Chill. Generous serving for 10

Lemon-Cheese Salad

1 pkg. lemon gelatin　　　1 pkg. lime gelatin
1½ cups water for lemon gelatin　½ cup fresh lemon
2 cups water for lime gelatin　　　juice
1 16 oz pkg. cream cheese　3 Tbsp. mayonnaise
　　1 small can crushed pineapple

Dissolve lemon gelatin in fresh juice and 1½ cups water. Chill until partially set. Cream cheese with mayonnaise and pineapple; fold in partially set gelatin and chill until set. Dissolve 1 pkg. lime gelatin in 2 cups hot water. Cool. Pour over set gelatin Chill until set.

Baked Bean Salad

can of pork & beans   chopped celery
onions   hard boiled egg slices
          lettuce for garnish

I was first introduced to this salad in Saratoga where it was a favorite dish around which to build a "hurry up" luncheon. The pork and beans are removed from the can and allowed to chill. They are mixed with finely chopped celery and onions---- served on lettuce and topped with hard boiled egg slices. To round out the luncheon, serve with brown bread & butter, iced tea, & gelatin topped with whipped cream. Most of this can be prepared at breakfast or night before.

Tomatoe-Cheese Salad

1 can Tomatoe soup (heated)   1/4 teasp. salt
1 pkg. lemon gelatin   1 pkg. cream cheese
1/4 cup vinegar   1 1/4 cups water
1/8 teasp. pepper   small amts. onions, celery
                              & bell pepper

Dissolve gelatin in water as directed on box and mix well with can of hot tomatoe soup, salt, pepper, and vinegar. Let cool and chill until partially set. Mix with other ingredients and chill again until firm. Serve on lettuce leaf.

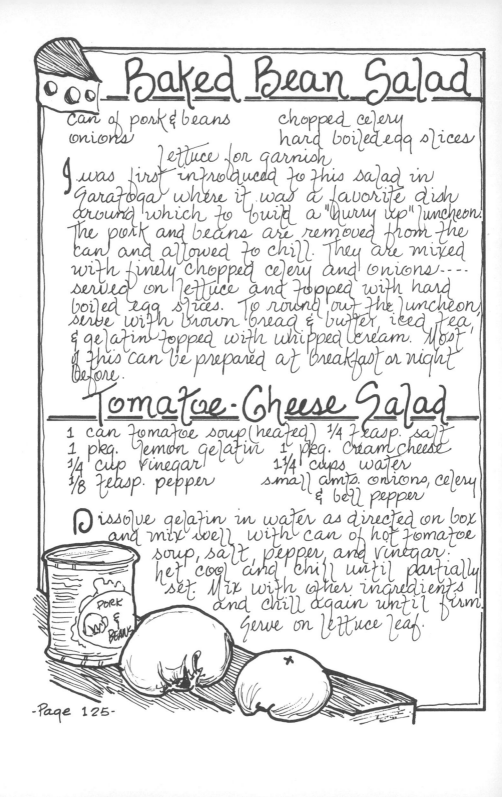

PORK & BEANS

Health Salad

3 large apples 1 cup grated carrots
½ cup raisins ½ cup chopped nut meats
½ cup diced celery pinch of salt
pinch of sugar

Dice apples in bowl. Add carrots, raisins, nut meats, and celery. Mix this with your favorite salad dressing. Add pinch of salt and sugar to taste.

Apple Vegetable Salad

2 cups of red or green apples (or both), peeled & diced
2 Tbsp. cider vinegar 1 cup shredded carrots
3 stalks celery (chopped) 1 teasp. sugar
mayonnaise lettuce · ½ teasp salt

Sprinkle apples with vinegar and let set a few minutes. Add all other ingredients except mayonnaise. Mix well. Moisten slightly with mayonnaise. Serve on lettuce leaf. Garnish with mayonnaise.

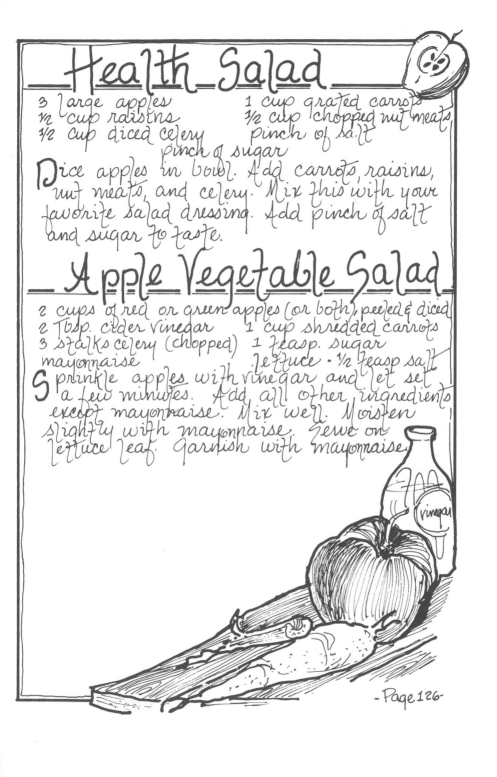

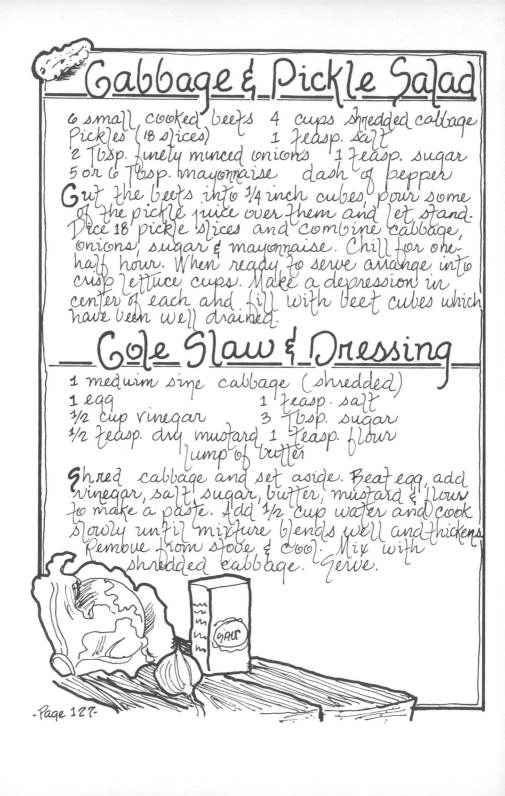

Cabbage & Pickle Salad

6 small cooked beets   4 cups shredded cabbage
Pickles (18 slices)   1 Teasp. salt
2 Tbsp. finely minced onions   1 Teasp. sugar
5 or 6 Tbsp. mayonnaise   dash of pepper

Cut the beets into 1/4 inch cubes, pour some of the pickle juice over them and let stand. Dice 18 pickle slices and combine cabbage, onions, sugar & mayonnaise. Chill for one-half hour. When ready to serve arrange into crisp lettuce cups. Make a depression in center of each and fill with beet cubes which have been well drained.

Cole Slaw & Dressing

1 meduim size cabbage (shredded)
1 egg   1 Teasp. salt
1/2 cup vinegar   3 Tbsp. sugar
1/2 Teasp. dry mustard 1 Teasp. flour
            lump of butter

Shred cabbage and set aside. Beat egg, add vinegar, salt, sugar, butter, mustard & flour to make a paste. Add 1/2 cup water and cook slowly until mixture blends well and thickens. Remove from stove & cool. Mix with shredded cabbage. Serve.

Catfish Stew

3 lbs. catfish   ½ lb. butts meat
1½ lb. potatoes   ¼ lb. onions
1 small can tomatoe soup.   ¼ lb. butter
      salt and pepper

Dice butts meat and fry for grease. Then add potatoes and onions to meat grease & cook until done, leaving little crisp bits of meat in mixture. Place these in rather large stew pot and add fish, soup, butter salt, & pepper and a little water. When this comes to a boil let it boil for about 20 minutes and serve.
(Butts meat is a form of fat back)
For hot stew add a little hot sauce.

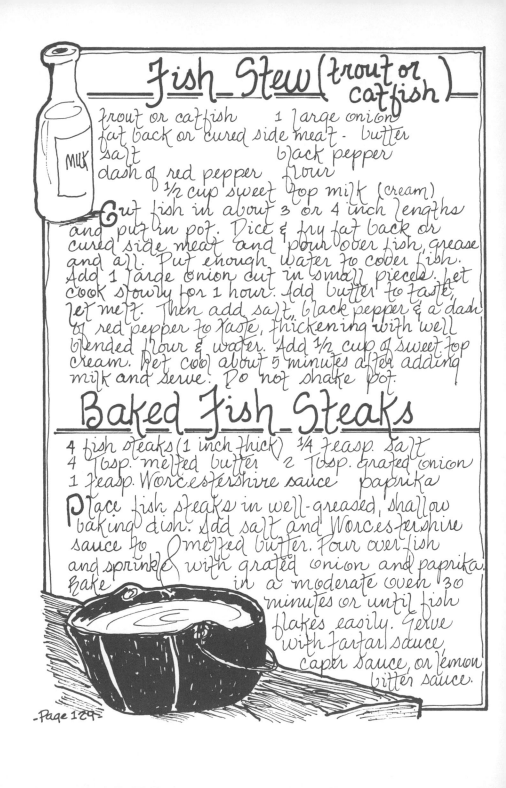

Fish Stew (trout or catfish)

trout or catfish   1 large onion
fat back or cured side meat - butter
salt   black pepper
dash of red pepper   flour
          ½ cup sweet top milk (cream)

Cut fish in about 3 or 4 inch lengths and put in pot. Dice & fry fat back or cured side meat and pour over fish, grease and all. Put enough water to cover fish. Add 1 large onion cut in small pieces. Let cook slowly for 1 hour. Add butter to taste, let melt. Then add salt, black pepper & a dash of red pepper to taste, thickening with well blended flour & water. Add ½ cup of sweet top cream. Let cook about 5 minutes after adding milk and serve. Do not shake pot.

Baked Fish Steaks

4 fish steaks (1 inch thick)   ¼ teasp. salt
4 Tbsp. melted butter   2 Tbsp. grated onion
1 teasp. Worcestershire sauce   paprika

Place fish steaks in well-greased, shallow baking dish. Add salt and Worcestershire sauce to melted butter. Pour over fish and sprinkle with grated onion and paprika. Bake in a moderate oven 30 minutes or until fish flakes easily. Serve with tartar sauce, caper sauce, or lemon butter sauce.

Curried Shrimp

1 onion	1 cup chopped apples
2 teasp. curry powder	1 cup milk
2 cups boiled shrimp	2 teasp. flour
to increase quanity	1 can chinese vegetables
may be added.	

Brown apple, onion, & shrimp in butter and cook until tender. Add curry powder & blend in flour-milk mixture. Simmer until served. Serve on rice with India Chutney (onions cut up and sprinkled with hot sauce) --- also shredded coconut and nuts.

Fried Shrimp

uncooked shrimp	sprinkle of salt
1 beaten egg	1 Tbsp. cold water
cracker crumbs	

Peel uncooked shrimp, leaving tail & removing black vein running down the back with knife, and wash. Sprinkle with a little salt. Combine 1 beaten egg with tablespoon cold water. Dip shrimp in egg mixture, then roll in finely crushed cracker crumbs. Fry in deep fat until golden brown. Drain on crumpled paper toweling. Good with hush puppies.

Oyster Fritters

1 pt. oysters   2 eggs
1/3 cup milk   1 1/3 cups flour
2 teasp. baking powder 1/2 tedsp. salt
          few grains pepper

Drain oysters and remove any bits of shell.
Chop oysters. Beat eggs and add milk.
Sift together flour, baking powder, salt &
pepper. Add milk mixture. Add oysters and
mix well. Drop by spoonfuls into shallow
fat (375°F.) Fry 3 minutes or until brown.
Drain on absorbent paper.

Oyster Pie

2 doz. oysters   1/2 cup of oyster liquor
1 box oysterettes   1/3 cup butter
2 well beaten eggs   1 cup sweet milk
          salt & pepper to taste

Put one layer of oysters in pan. Next
add one layer of crackers and then
one layer of oysters and so on until
all are used, then pour oyster liquor
eggs, and milk mixture over top,
dotting with butter   and
bake in moderate oven for
25 minutes or until done (350°F)

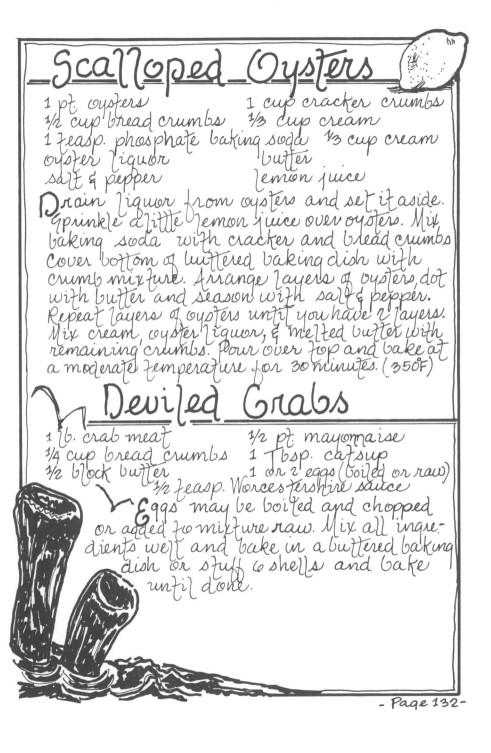

Scalloped Oysters

1 pt. oysters

½ cup bread crumbs

1 teasp. phosphate baking soda

oyster liquor

salt & pepper

1 cup cracker crumbs

⅓ cup cream

⅓ cup cream

butter

lemon juice

Drain liquor from oysters and set it aside. Sprinkle a little lemon juice over oysters. Mix baking soda with cracker and bread crumbs. Cover bottom of buttered baking dish with crumb mixture. Arrange layers of oysters, dot with butter and season with salt & pepper. Repeat layers of oysters until you have 2 layers. Mix cream, oyster liquor, & melted butter with remaining crumbs. Pour over top and bake at a moderate temperature for 30 minutes. (350°F)

Deviled Crabs

1 lb. crab meat

¼ cup bread crumbs

½ block butter

½ pt. mayonnaise

1 Tbsp. catsup

1 or 2 eggs (boiled or raw)

½ teasp. Worcestershire sauce

Eggs may be boiled and chopped or added to mixture raw. Mix all ingredients well and bake in a buttered baking dish or stuff 6 shells and bake until done.

Salmon Patties

1 beaten egg
1/4 teasp. salt
dash of pepper
1/2 cup quick oats

1 cup flaked salmon
1/4 teasp. paprika
1/3 cup milk
1/2 teasp. Worcestershire sauce

Combine all ingredients thoroughly. Salmon juice may be substituted for part of milk. Shape into patties and pan fry until golden brown.

Scalloped Salmon And Mushrooms

1 can salmon (1 lb.)
*1 can condensed mushroom soup (10½ ounces)
1 Tbsp. minced onion
1/2 cup cracker crumbs

1/2 cup top milk (or cream)
1 Tbsp. chopped parsley
1/2 cup grated cheese if desired

Drain salmon and remove skin and bones. Separate into large pieces and place into a greased porcelain baking pan. Mix soup, milk, onions, & parsley and pour over salmon. Sprinkle with cracker crumbs and grated cheese. Bake in a moderate oven (350°F.) for 15 to 20 minutes or until topping is browned. Makes about 5 servings.
*(canned mushroom soup substituted in original recipe.)

Pressed Chicken

1 chicken   salt & pepper

6 eggs   1 Tbsp. gelatin to each pint of broth.

Cook chicken well done. Cut fine, separating
the white meat from the dark. Hard boil the
eggs. Mash fine the yolks & the whites keeping
them separate. Salt and pepper. Soften gelatin in 2 tablespoons of water for each tablespoon of gelatin and add to the boiling
chicken broth. Place meat in dish, dark
layer first, then layer of mashed yolks, of white
meat, and finally layer of egg whites, adding
from time to time a little broth to moisten well.
When all is in dish, pour over it enough broth-
gelatin mixture to cover top. Chill until firm,
cut into slices and serve on lettuce leaves with or
without mayonnaise

Oven Fried Chicken

Chicken   salt
flour   pepper

Preheat oven to 350°F. Take frying chicken, cut
in pieces and wipe dry. Flour, salt and
pepper should be placed in paper bag.
Then drop the chicken in & shake a few
times to coat with flour. (do this a
few pieces at a time) Heat ½
inch layer of fat in heavy
frying pan. Brown chicken
on all sides with
unit turned to
fast. Place in cover-
ed casserole in
oven to
bake

Smothered Chicken & Rice

Once someone heard about having smothered chicken to eat and put their chicken under something and smothered it to death. Now please don't do that, but just kill it in the usual way. Do not use an old hen or rooster or a fryer, but a young hen, hardly grown will be fine. After it is cut up, sprinkle salt over it, to what you think will best suit your taste. Put chicken on in boiling or real hot water and add a few spoonfuls of fresh fried bacon grease - that is do not use old grease. Try to use enough water at the beginning to finish cooking the chicken. Do not boil extra fast but after cooking a reasonable time be sure the chicken is real tender and before setting it off the stove, you may fix a filling using a little cold water, a few spoonfuls of flour, a small amount of black pepper and stir this together before putting with the chicken. Use a little salt if needed to suit your taste --- then let it cook a few minutes before setting off the fire. Now you are ready to prepare your rice. Use a double boiler and long grain rice and put it on in boiling water. Have water a lite above the rice and salted to what you think will suit your taste and never stir it. Be sure to keep plenty of water in boiler under rice until done. After it is done do not allow to keep fully closed on account of sweating. (This quaint little recipe is presented to you exactly as we found it.)

The Editors

Chicken Pie

1 lb. chicken (boiled tender)   3 boiled eggs (chopped)
2 Tbsp. butter   chicken broth

Make crust with flour as usual. Chop eggs. Line a baking dish with crust. Put a layer of chicken, a layer of eggs, a layer of dumplings. Then pour chicken broth over it. Season with butter. Bake about 30 minutes at 400°F.

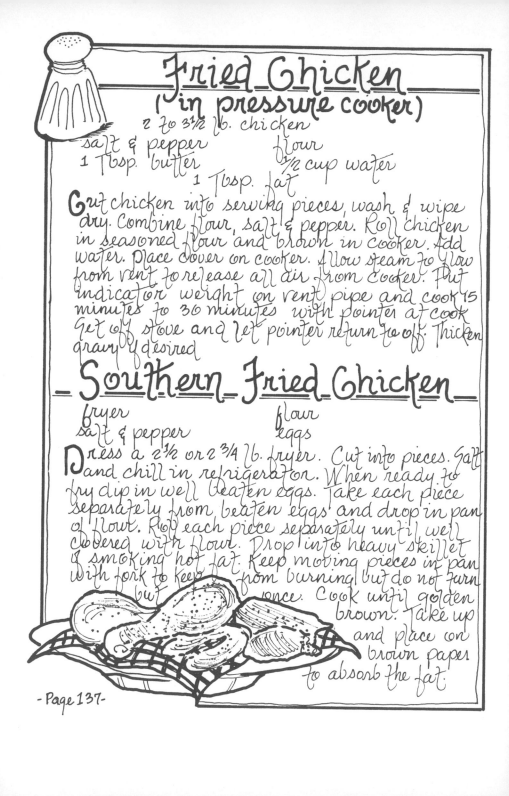

Fried Chicken
("in pressure cooker)

2 to 3½ lb. chicken
salt & pepper   flour
1 Tbsp. butter   ½ cup water
          1 Tbsp. fat

Cut chicken into serving pieces, wash & wipe dry. Combine flour, salt & pepper. Roll chicken in seasoned flour and brown in cooker. Add water. Place cover on cooker. Allow steam to flow from vent to release all air from cooker. Put indicator weight on vent pipe and cook 15 minutes to 30 minutes with pointer at cook. Get off stove and let pointer return to off. Thicken gravy if desired

Southern Fried Chicken

fryer   flour
salt & pepper   eggs

Dress a 2½ or 2¾ lb. fryer. Cut into pieces. Salt and chill in refrigerator. When ready to fry dip in well beaten eggs. Take each piece separately from beaten eggs and drop in pan of flour. Roll each piece separately until well covered with flour. Drop into heavy skillet & smoking hot fat. Keep moving pieces in pan with fork to keep from burning but do not turn but once. Cook until golden brown. Take up and place on brown paper to absorb the fat.

Creamed Chicken
(for the Family)

1 hen
1 cup chopped almonds
3 green peppers
1/2 cup cream
salt & cayenne pepper
4 Tbsp. flour

1 can mushrooms
yolks of 4 eggs
2 pimentoes
2 cups white sauce
4 Tbsp. of butter
1 cup chicken stock

Cook chicken until tender, but still firm. Make a white sauce as follows: Melt four tablespoons butter. Blend in gradually flour, cream, & chicken stock. Cook over boiling water stirring constantly until desired consistancy, add salt & pepper. This makes 2 cups white sauce. Cut the chicken into small pieces or slices. Dice the peppers fine. Add peppers, almonds, & mushrooms to sauce (filling for toast or pie shells). Sauce: Beat the egg yolks, stir in the cream & heat in double boiler over boiling water. Use this sauce over the chicken. Heat over hot water when ready to serve on toast or baked pastry shells. (Chicken may be placed in shells and sauce poured over while hot or chicken & sauce can be mixed & heated when ready to serve.

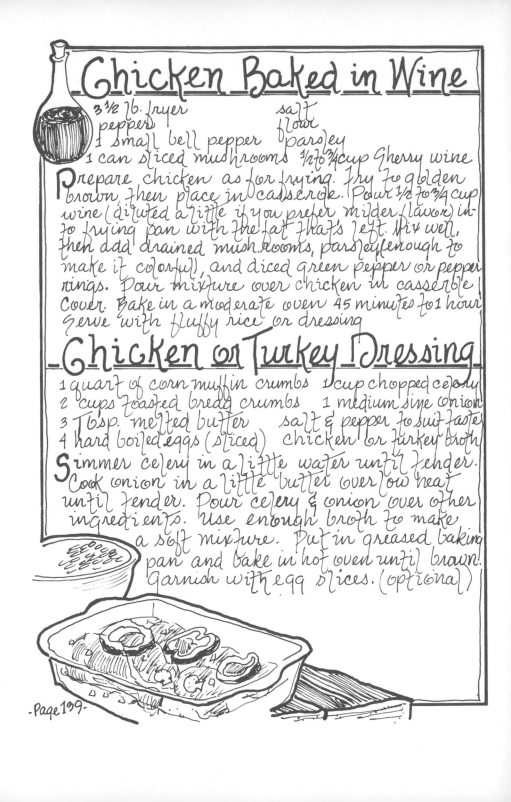

Chicken Baked in Wine

3 ½ lb. fryer   salt
pepper   flour
1 small bell pepper   parsley
1 can sliced mushrooms ½ to ¾ cup Sherry wine

Prepare chicken as for frying. Fry to golden brown, then place in casserole. Pour ½ to ¾ cup wine (diluted a little if you prefer milder flavor) into frying pan with the fat that's left. Mix well, then add drained mushrooms, parsley (enough to make it colorful), and diced green pepper or pepper rings. Pour mixture over chicken in casserole. Cover. Bake in a moderate oven 45 minutes to 1 hour. Serve with fluffy rice or dressing

Chicken or Turkey Dressing

1 quart of corn muffin crumbs 1 cup chopped celery
2 cups toasted bread crumbs 1 medium size onion
3 Tbsp. melted butter   salt & pepper to suit taste
4 hard boiled eggs (sliced) chicken or turkey broth

Simmer celery in a little water until tender. Cook onion in a little butter over low heat until tender. Pour celery & onion over other ingredients. Use enough broth to make a soft mixture. Put in greased baking pan and bake in hot oven until brown. Garnish with egg slices. (optional)

Home Cooked Brunswick (stew)

1 large hen or rooster   1 lb. butter beans
2 lbs. Irish potatoes (sliced) 1 lg. sine can tomatoes
1 large sine can corn or same amt. fresh corn
½ lb good fresh butter   salt & pepper to taste
lemon juice to taste   hot pepper to taste if desired

Clean and cut up chicken and cook till tender and will fall from bones. Meanwhile, cook butter beans, onions, and potatoes in very little water until well done. Add these vegetables to the chicken. Also add butter (unless the chicken is very fat.), corn, and tomatoes last. Season to taste with salt, pepper & lemon juice Cook very slowly, stirring often until very thick. Add hot pepper to taste if desired.

Barbecued Chicken

chickens   salt & pepper

Split chickens down back. Salt & pepper lightly. Place chickens in biscuit pan inside down in an open about 350°F. When meat begins to brown baste with sauce
2 teasp. salt - 2 teasp. pepper - 1 Tbsp. dry mustard
1½ Tbsp. sugar - ½ Tbsp. red pepper ½ stick butter
1 cup juice from chickens - 5 Tbsp. vinegar
3 Tbsp. Worcestershire sauce

Mix the dry ingredients well. Add enough water to make a paste. Add vinegar, Worcestershire sauce, butter & juice from chickens. Stir and heat over low flame until butter melts Pour over chickens baste often.

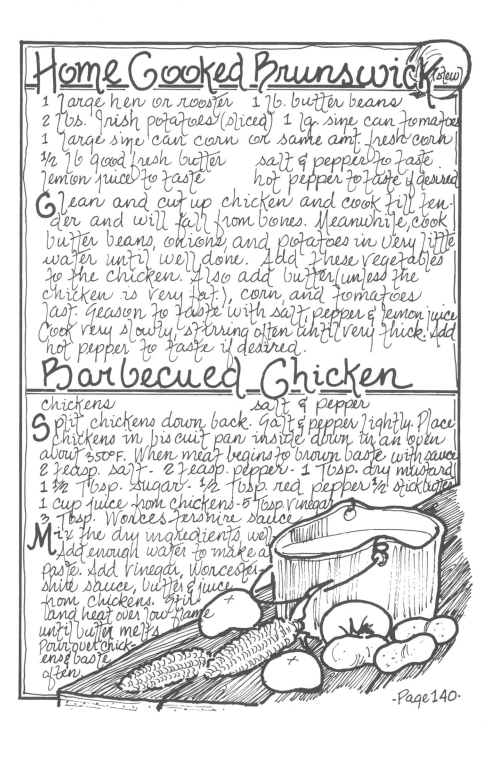

Country Captain

1 hen (4 lbs. or more)	1 bunch celery
2 green peppers	4 large onions
1 button garlic	1 can tomatoes
3/4 cup currants	1 can pimentos
small amt. Worcestershire	salt & pepper

1 Tbsp. curry powder.

The hen may be baked or stewed. Boil or bake hen until tender. If hen is boiled, all the ingredients are chopped and placed in the pot with the hen to simmer until tender, adding currants last. If the hen is baked and you want a lovely attractive dish, place whole onions, sliced peppers & celery sticks around baking hen until tender, then add other ingredients, saving currants until last. Hen may be cut up or left whole, as desired.

Mock Drumsticks

1/2 lb. ground beef chuck	1/2 lb. ground veal shoulder
3/4 teasp. salt	1/8 teasp. pepper
1/2 teasp. sage	2 teasp. chopped onion
dry crumbs	

Combine beef, veal, salt, pepper, sage, & onion. Mix well and shape like drumsticks. Roll in crumbs. Fry in shallow fat 10 minutes. Drain on absorbent paper. Insert wooden skewers. Place paper frills on skewers. Serves 4.

Barbecued Burgers

1 lb. ground beef	1 cup chopped onion
½ cup celery (diced)	¼ cup shortening
¼ cup catsup.	1 cup cooked tomatoes
1 cup water	2 teasp. salt
¼ teasp pepper	1 teasp. chili powder

toasted rolls

Lightly brown ground beef, onions, & celery in shortening. Add remaining ingredients. Cover and cook over low heat about 20 minutes. Serve on toasted rolls.

Beef Stroganoff

2 lbs. round steak, cut into ½ inch cubes
1 large onion, sliced   1 pt. sour cream
1 can mushrooms   salt & pepper to taste
rice   2 Tbsp heavy brown soy sauce

Brown onions in butter (or any fat) Dredge meat in flour and brown. Add other ingredients. Serve over rice as main dish for meal.

Stuffed Pork Chops

Casserole or thrift cooker   ½ cup hot water
6 rib pork chops 1½ inch thick (with pocket)
1½ cups whole wheat bread (break) 2 Tbsp celery
2 Tbsp. onion   salt & pepper
2 Tbsp. butter   ¼ cup flour
         ½ teasp. mustard

Moisten bread with water. Add minced celery, minced onion, salt & pepper to suit taste and butter. Fill pocket of pork chop with this mixture and fasten securely. Mix together flour and mustard. Dip chops in flour mixture and brown in shortening. Arrange chops in casserole or on rack of thrift cooker adding 1 cup water. Cover & bake or steam. Veal or lamb may be used in place of pork. Bake at 350°F for 1½ hours.

Braised Lamb Chops

4 lamb shoulder chops   salt & pepper
4 lemon slices   4 thin slices of onion
4 green pepper rings   ½ cup Tabasco sauce

Brown seasoned chops well in hot fat. Top each chop with a slice of lemon, a slice of onion, and a green pepper ring. Add Tabasco sauce, cover and cook slowly for 40 minutes or 45 minutes. Serves 4

Meat Loaf I

1 lb. ground beef	½ lb. ground pork
½ lb. ground veal	2 teasp. salt
½ teasp. pepper	1 cup bread crumbs
¼ cup butter	½ cup minced onions
½ cup minced celery	1 egg in ½ cup milk

Have meat ground twice. Brown the onions in butter and add the milk. Add bread crumbs & seasoning to meat. Then add the milk mixture to meat. Mix well. Pack in a buttered pan or form into a loaf. Arrange strips of bacon over the loaf & bake until done.

Meat Loaf II

1 lb. ground beef	1 cup bread crumbs
1 teasp. salt	2 teasp. pepper
1 Tbsp. vinegar	½ cup milk
½ cup catsup	1 egg

Soak bread crumbs in milk about 15 minutes. Add ground beef, salt, pepper, egg, vinegar, and catsup. Mix well. Shape into a loaf and put into a greased pan. Bake in oven at 400°F. until firm and well browned.

Welsh Rarebit

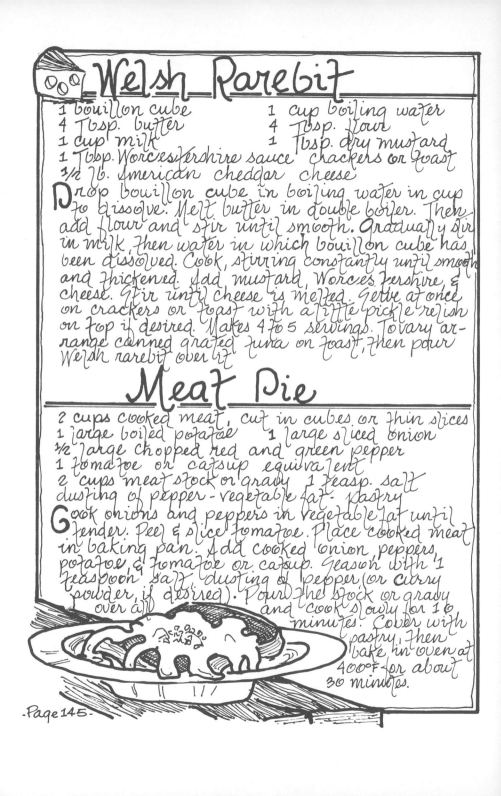

1 bouillon cube   1 cup boiling water
4 Tbsp. butter   4 Tbsp. flour
1 cup milk   1 Tbsp. dry mustard
1 Tbsp. Worcestershire sauce   crackers or toast
½ lb. American cheddar cheese

Drop bouillon cube in boiling water in cup to dissolve. Melt butter in double boiler. Then add flour and stir until smooth. Gradually stir in milk, then water in which bouillon cube has been dissolved. Cook, stirring constantly until smooth and thickened. Add mustard, Worcestershire, & cheese. Stir until cheese is melted. Serve at once on crackers or toast with a little pickle relish on top if desired. Makes 4 to 5 servings. To vary arrange canned grated tuna on toast, then pour Welsh rarebit over it.

Meat Pie

2 cups cooked meat, cut in cubes or thin slices
1 large boiled potatoe   1 large sliced onion
½ large chopped red and green pepper
1 tomatoe or catsup equivalent
2 cups meat stock or gravy   1 teasp. salt
dusting of pepper - vegetable fat - pastry

Cook onions and peppers in vegetable fat until tender. Peel & slice tomatoe. Place cooked meat in baking pan. Add cooked onion, peppers, potatoe, & tomatoe or catsup. Season with 1 teaspoon salt, dusting of pepper (or curry powder, if desired). Pour the stock or gravy over all and cook slowly for 10 minutes. Cover with pastry, then bake in oven at 400°F for about 30 minutes.

Ham Salad Sandwich

2 cups finely chopped ham
1/4 cup chopped sweet pickle   2 Tbsp prepared mustard
mayonnaise or salad dressing   2 sliced tomatoes
4 lettuce leaves · 8 slices bread · butter to taste

Combine ham, pickle & mustard. Moisten to spreading consistancy with mayonnaise. Add generous layers of filling to 4 slices of buttered bread &
top with tomato slices & lettuce. Makes 4 sandwiches.

My Favorite Boiled Ham

ham   1 teasp. brown sugar
1 teasp. spiced vinegar   Cloves
several dashes catsup.   salt & pepper

Place ham or shoulder in boiler half full of water.
Season with 1 teaspoon each of brown sugar
and spiced vinegar. Cook slowly until well done,
then remove the skin and top with cloves.
Sprinkle with brown sugar, spiced vinegar &
dashes of catsup. Brown in medium hot oven
until top of ham is golden crisp, then remove to
a rack & allow to drip until cold enough to slice evenly.

Cheese & Ham Appetizers

2 Tbsp. mayonnaise   2 Tbsp. chopped stuffed
1/2 teasp. prepared mustard   Olives
1 pkg. soft cream cheese   4 thin slices cold boiled
                                - ham

Blend first 4 ingredients &
spread 1/8 inch thick over
ham slices. Roll ham jelly roll
fashion, fasten with toothpicks
& chill 1 hour. Then with
very sharp knife, cut
roll in 1/4 inch slices.
Place on small
crackers & serve
with chilled to-
mato juice.

Ham Loaf Bettina

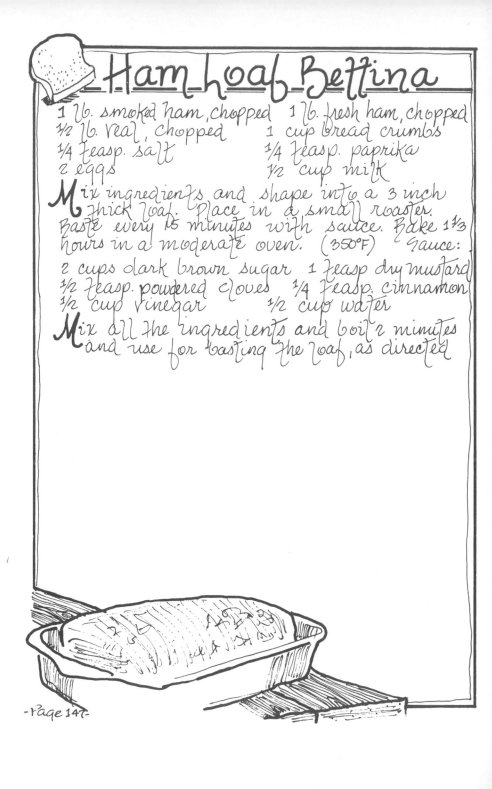

1 lb. smoked ham, chopped   1 lb. fresh ham, chopped
½ lb. veal, chopped   1 cup bread crumbs
¼ teasp. salt   ¼ teasp. paprika
2 eggs   ½ cup milk

Mix ingredients and shape into a 3 inch thick loaf. Place in a small roaster. Baste every 15 minutes with sauce. Bake 1⅓ hours in a moderate oven. (350°F)   Sauce:

2 cups dark brown sugar   1 teasp dry mustard
½ teasp. powdered cloves   ¼ teasp. cinnamon
½ cup vinegar   ½ cup water

Mix all the ingredients and boil 2 minutes and use for basting the loaf, as directed

Spaghetti & Meat Balls

1 medium sized onion, finely chopped
½ lb. choice ground beef   1 can tomato sauce
1 green bell pepper, finely chopped dash of paprika
salt & pepper to taste   spaghetti
2 dashes of liquid red pepper sauce
1 teasp. Worcestershire sauce

Into slightly greased fry pan, put one medium sized onion, finely chopped. Cook until medium brown, not hard, stirring constantly to separate pieces of meat and prevent lumping. To this add one green bell pepper, finely chopped, and cook for 1 minute, stirring constantly. To this add 1 can of tomato sauce, a dash of paprika, 1 teaspoon Worcestershire sauce, 2 dashes of liquid red pepper sauce, salt & pepper to taste. Continue stirring while it simmers for 5 minutes over low heat. Serve this over spaghetti or place in separate plates and mix as desired. If a Chinese flavor is desired, add 1½ teaspoons of soy sauce and 1 cup of cooked rice instead of spaghetti. To make meat balls, roll meat, onions, bell pepper up together in little balls and fry till medium brown. Mix all other ingredients and pour over meat balls. Simmer till flavor is absorbed. A little water may be added to both these methods if thinner sauce is desired. Spaghetti should be cooked in boiling salted water until tender as desired.

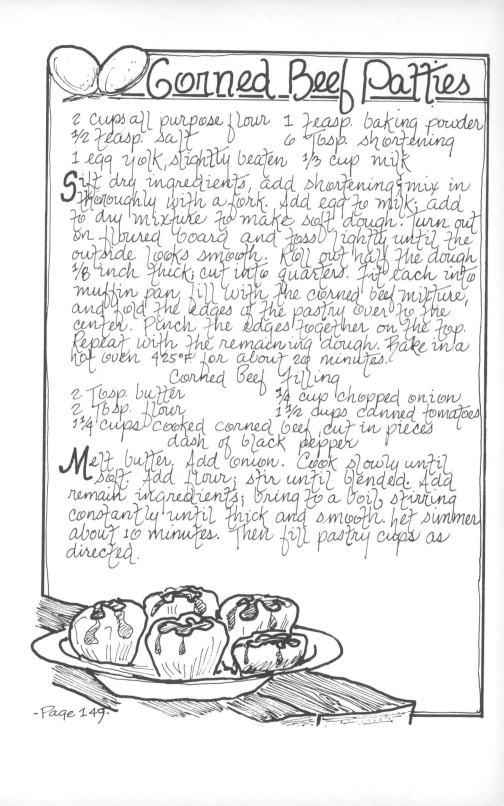

Corned Beef Patties

2 cups all purpose flour   1 teasp. baking powder
1/2 teasp. salt   6 Tbsp. shortening
1 egg yolk, slightly beaten 1/3 cup milk

Sift dry ingredients, add shortening & mix in thoroughly with a fork. Add egg to milk; add to dry mixture to make soft dough. Turn out on floured board and toss lightly until the outside looks smooth. Roll out half the dough 1/8 inch thick; cut into quarters. Fit each into muffin pan, fill with the corned beef mixture, and fold the edges of the pastry over to the center. Pinch the edges together on the top. Repeat with the remaining dough. Bake in a hot oven 425°F for about 20 minutes.

Corned Beef Filling

2 Tbsp. butter   1/4 cup chopped onion
2 Tbsp. flour   1 1/2 cups canned tomatoes
1 1/4 cups cooked corned beef, cut in pieces
dash of black pepper

Melt butter. Add onion. Cook slowly until soft. Add flour; stir until blended. Add remain ingredients; bring to a boil, stirring constantly until thick and smooth. Let simmer about 10 minutes. Then fill pastry cups as directed.

Basic Measurements

3 Teaspoons	1 Tablespoon
4 Tablespoons	1/4 cup
5 Tablespoons plus 1 Teaspoon	1/3 cup
8 Tablespoons	1/2 cup
10 Tablespoons plus 2 Teaspoons	2/3 cup
12 Tablespoons	3/4 cup
16 Tablespoons	1 cup
2 cups	1 pint
2 pints	1 quart
1/4 pound butter	1/2 cup
1 square chocolate	1 ounce

Table of Equivalent Weights & Measures

1 salt spoon	1/4 teaspoon
3 Teaspoons	1 Tablespoon
16 Tablespoons	1 cup
2 cups	1 pint
2 pints	1 quart
4 cups	1 quart
2 cups butter	1 pound
2 cups granulated sugar	1 pound
4 cups flour	1 pound
2 Tablespoons liquid	1 ounce
2 Tablespoons butter	1 ounce
4 Tablespoons flour	1 ounce
1 square unsweetened chocolate	1 ounce
3 1/2 Tablespoon cocoa	1 ounce

Helpful Cooking Tips

A. Cooking Tips on fruit:
  1. In cooking acid fruits, the addition of 1/4 teasp. of baking soda will reduce acidity and it also reduces the amount of sugar to be added to one-half.
  2. Before starting to cook jam, rub the inside of the pot with a little salad oil and it will not stick.
  3. To keep bananas from turning dark on cake or salad, add a few drops of lemon juice to them.

B. Cooking Tips on Vegetables:
  1. It is important that canned & glassed vegetables be heated in their liquor to conserve the food value that dissolves out into liquor.
  2. To thoroughly clean greens of any kind, wash in warm water twice, letting stand 3 to 4 minutes. Then freshen in cold water.
  3. How to cook vegetables.
  (a) Root Vegetables   start in cold water with sea-
      (beneath ground)   sonings & cover.
  (b) Green Vegetables   start in boiling water
      (above ground)   with seasonings & do not cover
  4. When cooking strong smelling vegetables such as collards, cabbages, rutabagas, & meats add 2 or 3 pecan meats to pot to reduce strong odor.

C. Cooking Tips on butter:
  1. To measure butter, fill the measuring cup with water then use amount of butter. For instance if recipe calls for 1/4 cup butter, fill cup 3/4 full of water & add butter until the water reaches 1 cup level, etc.
  2. A thin coating of butter over cut cheese keeps the cut surfaces of cheese moist

D. Cooking Tip on Tea
  1. A little boiling water added to cloudy tea will clear the beverage.

E. Cooking Tip on egg yolks.
  1. To keep leftover egg yolks from getting hard, cover them with water & leave it 'til time for use.

Helpful Cooking Tips (continued)

7. Cooking tips on ground meat:
   1. Before making out ground meat patties wet hands in cold water & do not dry & the meat will not stick to hands.

9. Cooking tips on pie crust:
   1. Cool pies on rack so bottom won't get soggy.
   2. Instead of pricking a precooked pie shell to make it cook flat, set a smaller pie plate on pie crust while cooking.

* Household Hint

1. To keep clothes from freezing on line in freezing weather, add 1 cup salt to last rinsing water

* This little household hint had nothing whatsoever to do with cooking other than the fact that it was listed among the other tips. We felt it quaint enough to include.

The Editors

C.H.